Eternal Life.

Yes, Forever!

Written by

mike hillebrecht

Eternal Life. Yes, Forever!

ISBN-13 978-0615623542

ISBN-10 0615623549

Unless noted otherwise all scripture quotations are from the King James Bible.

Due to the dynamic nature of the Internet, any website address or link contained within this book may have changed and no longer be valid.

If you're looking for more information, feel free to join the discussion at: www.lifeyesforever.com

Published by

Charis Academy Publishing

Portland, Oregon

www.charisacademy.org

More books by mike hillebrecht

Grace for Shame

Chesed – Beyond the Veil of Mercy

Your Life is a Freaking Mess and You Want Answers

A Kingdom Primer

Eternal Life.

Dedicated to every
forerunner that continues
to set the mark and challenge those who follow.
Let this mind be in you, too.

Eternal Life.

Contents

Eternal Life.

Preface

On an early Sunday morning, I sat contemplating and meditating the prophetic word spoken over me from the proceeding night's service. It was about a series of writings which I would be undertaking which would make a great impact in the world. My wife and I had spoken late into the night about what these writings were to encompass. As I sipped my coffee, I opened up the book I had been reading called, *The Pleasures of God* by John Piper. What I read in this opening paragraph to the fifth chapter was confirmation to me about what I was about to undertake.

"Can controversial teachings nurture Christlikeness? *Before you answer this question, ask another one: Are there any significant biblical teachings that have not been controversial? I cannot think of even one, let alone the number we all need for the daily nurture of faith. If this is true, then we have no choice but to seek our food in the markets of controversy. We need not stay there. We can go home and feast if the day has been well spent. But we must buy there. As much as we would like it, we do not have the luxury of living in a world where the most nourishing truths are unopposed. If we think we can suspend judgment on all that is controversial and feed our souls only on what is left,*

we are living in a dream world. There is nothing left. The reason any of us think that we can stand alone on truths that are non-controversial is because we do not know our history or the diversity of the professing church. Besides that, would we really want to give to the devil the right to determine our spiritual menu by refusing to eat any teaching over which he can cause controversy?"[1]

The prophetical significance of this passage is that according to biblical teachings, the number five (the chapter I was reading from) represents grace, the very heavenly commodity I'll need to complete the task set before me. The declaration by an esteemed man of God about sound biblical teaching to be controversial only under girds the content which you are about to read and meditate upon. I could not have said it more clearly.

So what is the church controversy that I am about to illuminate? Death. Or better yet, resurrection, which, of course, leads to eternal life. Why is this controversial? Due to the fact that when you begin talking about eternal life and all its implications, there is a religious spirit who raises its head and says that you're making yourself to be like God. Jesus encountered it and with this reading you will encounter it too, not from me, but from the teachings that may have been planted in you or that you've developed all on your own. Let me assure you the word of God is very clear in what He thinks about you, and what your new nature is to be like. However, for man's

---

[1] John Piper, *The Pleasures of God*, Multnomah Press 1991

entire walk upon this planet, he has let the enemy whisper into his ear that he knows what is best for man; this has caused nothing but problems for believers. Simply, we aren't supposed to participate with the enemy and yet, for two thousand years, born-again/saved believers have embraced the life-giving nature of Christ, then ended it all by being taken out of this world by the enemy in order to reach a heavenly resting place. If you think this is right, why would the Creator of the universe use such a ruse to bring you into His presence? Maybe we need to rethink what Jesus did for us, gave to us, and how this free gift is to be used in these days.

> Hebrews 6:1-3 "Therefore **leaving the principles of the doctrine of Christ, let us go on unto perfection;** not laying again the foundation of repentance from dead works, and of faith toward God, Of the doctrine of baptisms, and of laying on of hands, and of **resurrection of the dead,** and of eternal judgment. And this will we do, if God permit."

My intent with these words is to help you break out of the constraints which have shackled your mind and every subsequent decision that you've made because of faulty thinking related to this area of living. I will try not to do it in a fashion that is preachy to the point of making you feel lower than maggot mud or to the other extreme of being too philosophically high-minded to the point of leaving you gasping for oxygen as your nose bleeds profusely in the rarified air of philosophy. I hope to present this just as I have been inspired to by the leading of Holy Spirit. If I come across as arrogant or brash at times, please pardon me from the understanding that I have a revelation which will not accept the responses of what has been before. As Paul said, "let this mind be in you..." I want you to have the mind of Christ in this subject too. As far as I know, the standard party line of teaching this material just doesn't cut it.

I will throughout this book make a few assumptions. The first being that you are ... well ... breathing. I say this because, to my recollection, no dead person has ever read anything I've written. This leads to my second assumption, that you can read and make an informed decision when presented with certain information. Fortunately this assumption leads to my third assumption that is if you don't have enough information to make an informed decision, you know how to find additional material to aid in the second assumption. This leads to my fourth, and final assumption that once you see the truth, you will do everything in your power to eliminate the ignorant thinking from your past and its results from your life so you can walk in the fullness of what God has predestined you to walk in.

As you'll notice in these assumptions, I do not care what your religious background is or your command of the Bible. I believe the reason you picked up this book was because you're not satisfied with your current reading material, since it doesn't seem to answer that nagging question you have burning inside of you. You know the question I'm talking about – the one that you never ask in church, but always ask in your car when you're pulling out of the parking lot. I intend within the context of this material to answer as many questions as I offer and raise many more that you'll need to find answers to. It is quite possible that if you picked this up to be refreshed, you may well leave thirstier than when you arrived. I will assure you of one thing: I'm not going to be the one teaching you anything here. That is the job of Holy Spirit. I am merely the vessel.

I must admit I will sometimes (okay, more often than not) use humor to put my point across. To some this might also appear to be rude and undignified. I don't do this out of disrespect for my readers but merely as a creative tool to lighten what many believe to be a terribly serious matter. Death and dying are very serious matters until you look at it through the eyes of God. Once you see what He has accomplished through His son, Jesus, and what our requirement is, you'll see that it's now no big deal. Really, no big deal – we make more of it than He ever intended us to.

Lastly, I do not seek the fame or recognition, good or bad, that this work may create. According to Matthew 6:33, "...seek ye first the Kingdom of God and His righteousness..." is what I'm seeking after. So please enjoy.

"Though all the winds of doctrine were let loose to play upon the Earth, so Truth be in the field, we do

injuriously by licensing and prohibiting to misdoubt her strength. Let her and Falsehood grapple; who ever knew Truth put to the worse, in a free and open encounter." John Milton

Uh Huh... I've heard that before.

*Mark 6:2-6 And when the sabbath day was come, he began to teach in the synagogue: and many hearing him were astonished, saying, From whence hath this man these things? and what wisdom is this which is given unto him, that even such mighty works are wrought by his hands? (3) Is not this the carpenter, the son of Mary, the brother of James, and Joses, and of Juda, and Simon? and are not his sisters here with us? And they were offended at him. (4) But Jesus said unto them, A prophet is not without honour, but in his own country, and among his own kin, and in his own house. (5) And he could there do no mighty work, save that he laid his hands upon a few sick folk, and healed them. (6) **And he marvelled because of their unbelief.** And he went round about the villages, teaching.*

Doubt. Unbelief. Offence. These are the three spirits that every new teaching must overcome in order to be accepted. Even the words which were spoken by Jesus, the very words from the throne of God, had to overcome these spiritual forces. So let's get it out of the way right up front. In love, for what I am about to say in these words, get over yourself. I mean don't think just because you've heard this before that it's not going to apply to you. Or, *"I can't believe what's being purported here as* 'truth' can be real because of what has happened in my life already." Or, "How dare he speak of such things in that manner; doesn't he know who I am, what I've been, or am going through?"

My singular response to this is: Grow up. This topic is not for those babes in Christ. You can find your binkie and enjoy your nap time in any of a number of churches across the globe with people who will cater to your Kingdom-toilet-training issues with a loving hand. But when you're ready to take on the business of your Father, you're going to have to leave the childish ways, and all their trappings, which include the mindsets you've created for yourself to help overcome the deficiencies that have not been demonstrated within the doctrine you have embraced. You are entering the throne zone.

This is pretty heady stuff here. Contained here within will be that most profaned "D-word", Death. Yes, the "D-word" will be repeated and alluded to numerous times and it will illicit deep guttural groanings from deep within you the likes of which you've never witnessed before. Death. It isn't a pleasant experience for anyone to undergo. The mere mention of it causes a hush to come over people. There is a sacredness to the word due to the impact of its actions, and people fear that talking about it will cause it to come near them. It is my hope that the ploy which it has cloaked itself in will be ripped asunder, and once finally exposed, you will realize the "D-word" really is a shadow of a very small mind in a brightly lit room.

Jesus stated that the tradition of man has made the word of God to no effect. This is still ringing true to this day as vast numbers of believers succumb to the ravages of an enemy who has successfully propagated the myth that dying is the culmination of a life dedicated to the Living God. Just because it has been going on for millenniums does not make it correct. The very funeral act, and all the ceremonial trappings which follow it, are an example of the traditions of man which Jesus spoke about. Clearly, this indicates that God's word is then made to no effect. How? What does the word of God say? Simply, you are an eternal being and don't have the characteristic that permits death to permeate your body.

Some of you might consider that this thinking isn't appropriate. Tell me, in light of what the Bible says, how should I think? You see I've been to funerals of the saved and unsaved, and frankly, there is no difference in how they are conducted. People come and surround a form that once was living but now has agreed to man's traditional way of thinking about life. Many cry and try to find solace in the memories of past events. Depending on the "goodness" of the person's character, there are those who will memorialize the departed, some more than others. All agree at the end, amid the snot and blubbering, that the person is in a better place.

"How can you in good conscience make these ..." Don't get bent out of shape. We need to stop allowing "good" from getting in the way of God. Jesus experienced this same attitude

with Jarius's daughter, with the widow from Naim, and even at the hands of the family of one of his friend's, Lazarus. Peter even experienced it with Tabitha. In every one of these cases, those mourning the loss were removed, even though they thought what they were doing was good. The "good" of man is tradition which has come from the fall of man when he partook from the tree of the knowledge of good and evil. Jesus said there is no one good except the Father. So I don't have a "good conscience" as much as I have a "God Conscience." And according to His thoughts, His word and His plan, you and I are eternal beings.

"Well, I know that," you may be thinking. This is what I'm now talking about. Your ability to form a response to a thought which appears to align with what you've heard the word of God says. However, your thought apparently lacks the power of an eternal being. Traditional thinking derived from years of religious manipulation is forcing you into a life that doesn't line up with what God says you are. Because no one ever told you how an eternal being is to operate, you've just gone on doing whatever you felt was supposed to be done. If preachers had spoken to you as often about being eternal as they preach on tithing I assure you that they wouldn't be concerned about their budgets every time one in "their flock" departs. But they can only reveal to you what they know works for them. Since they haven't "seen" eternal life, they have difficulty in preaching it to you. But the word of God says that those things which are seen are temporal while those things that are unseen are eternal. The

wisdom and logic of man will always describe that which is seen, while the wisdom and logic of that which comes from above will reveal that which isn't seen. After all, if you can see it, why does it need to be revealed?

Let me ask you this: How do you know that you're an eternal being? Most people these days believe they are eternal, just ask Oprah, she'll tell you. This is the question which will be addressed in these pages. I warn you, I will not answer it directly if that is what you're looking for. There is a discovery process that must occur if you are going not only to obtain this, but also retain it. It is one of those pearls in a field you must give all so that you'll have in order to possess.

All truths, once revealed, place upon us the impetus to correct fallacies we've embraced from previous generations. Often the folklore of these fallacies has become comfortable, and we've managed to live our lives because without their comfort we wouldn't have any signposts with which to base our journey. So the difficult task of constructing new signposts for a road you've never traveled can seem daunting, if not impossible. And I will agree with you here. In our humanity this task is impossible to navigate. It is likened unto Columbus setting out for the new world; he did not know how to get there but only that it had to exist, so he must find it the only way he knew how to, which was by relying on God to point him in the right direction. Let me begin to lead you off the path of traditional thinking towards the Kingdom of Heaven realm. From there God will take you on the rest of the way to what He intends for you in this journey.

Imagine one day in the future, for some strange reason, you die. You go to Heaven as you have always dreamed. There is the archangel, Gabriel, meeting people at the gates to the heavenly realm. As you approach, you notice loved ones that have gone on before in the distance waving and cheering as you near the gates of Heaven. Your attention becomes focused on the events which are unfolding before you as a small group of people are standing, waiting outside the gates. The expression on their faces seems to indicate that they are perplexed for some reason. As you watch them, one by one more people with the same expression begin to be added to this group while others walk through the gates of Heaven. Then you notice a rather large angel approach this group of bewildered saints along with a whole group of angels behind him. As the various angels pair off with the saints, the apparent lead angel directs the entire group towards a path which travels away from the gates of Heaven off into the distance. Trying to recall past accounts, you surmise that these must be those who will be cast into the lake of fire.

Now, your attention becomes focused on the gate of Heaven which looms ahead of you and the three people ahead of you. You overhear Gabriel ask each person their name and then examine a ledger in his hands. Placing a mark next to their name he instructs each one to pass through the gate after which they will be instructed by their guardian angel as to where they will be going and what will be happening to them. You approach as the last passes through the gate. "Name?" asks Gabriel. You state your name. He scans the roster before him with the aid of his marker. "Do you declare that Jesus Christ is your Lord and Savior?" he asks you. The oddity of this question is what causes you to pause. Not the question itself, just that it is asked to you in Heaven and you didn't hear it asked to the people before you. "Yes, I do," you respond with heart-felt assurance. "Good! Will you please proceed over to there," he says motioning over the place where you had previously seen those other people standing with the puzzled looks on their face. "May I inquire as to why? Have I done something wrong?" you anxiously ask. "Oh, there's nothing to be concerned about. You answered my question correctly, just as I knew you would. We clearly have it shown here that you have been a disciple of Jesus for a number of years on earth attending a number of gathering places of fellow disciples during that time. The works that you have done for the Lord are well recognized and deeply appreciated. Your dedication to Him is very admirable."

"But, I saw some people over there a moment ago and ... ", you begin as Gabriel starts crouching down near you. "Yes." he states in a rather hushed tone. "You need to know that we have a new policy which has come down from the Top. Basically, since you are a disciple of the Lord, it has been decided that the fullness of His life must be demonstrated back on earth. You and followers such as yourself are now being returned back to earth to begin where you left off. So you'll be returning to live until the fullness of time has occurred. Your first assignment when you arrive will be to tell those like yourself what changes have been made up here so that we don't have to go through this task so often. Thank you for your patience. Next." He says as he waves you on. "But what about those other people? Why did they get to go in?" you respond anxiously as you notice a pair of angels approaching you. "Yes, they were ones who hadn't heard the good news yet and we want to make sure they know what is going on here. This is all rather new for them you know. We don't want to see even one of them perish if we can help it. That's kind of what you'll be in charge of when you return. Please follow your guardian angel at this time and he'll direct you onto where you should be. Next."

Is it possible Heaven could become so filled with disciples before the fullness of time that it decides the fullness of the gospel has to be completed in the church as a prerequisite for the end of all time? How would you respond to such a mandate from Heaven should it happen to you? How would you change your focus if you were told this story from someone whose funeral you attended? Weird, isn't it?

In the eyes of many, Heaven has become the escape clause in the contract Christians hold with their Creator. I regret to tell you this, but He doesn't expect you to be there. I'll talk about this more as we go further. As you have probably determined, this is not going to be your "traditional" romp reading through the Bible. I intend to make you stop and take notice of the signposts that are missing in your journey - not to dismiss all you've encountered. Most journeys traveling forward seem to never have signposts, and if you see one, it simply means there has been someone before you who has come this way. Those markings are welcomed initially, but sooner or later, you're going to have to step out into a wilderness and become the pioneer God created you to be. That operation will defer many to the prevalent mode of thinking in church: WWJD.

What would Jesus do? We have reached a marketing saturation point for the WWJD symbolism to the point where it has diluted the very essence of the perfume it was designed to carry. If you are the carrier of the seed of Christ, the temple of the living God, have the mind of Christ and the Holy Spirit dwelling within you, why should you permit yourself the condemning task of consulting the dead nature in you to ask what the resident would do? Consider, the greater works you are to do, are just right in front of you, and your hesitation to "consult" with the Jesus-nature is the point where the plug to the power has been undone. John said that there would not be enough books to contain the things which Jesus did. Since all we know about Jesus is what is described in the four gospels, and much of it repeats itself, why don't you stop limiting yourself. Let's change the marketing to: JDIJD. Just do it. Jesus did.

A bath or rescued from drowning.

How would you feel if someone you didn't even know - maybe in the supermarket or at work or even across from your house - started calling you names? Let's say it's three people at each of these locations and each one calls you the same name. You didn't do anything to them, you've never even spoke to them. And yet they call you this name. And it's not once that they call you this, but many times. Soon they are telling their friends and family members about you and they're even starting to call you by this name. You begin to notice that when you're in the checkout lane at the grocery store a couple of people a few aisles away seem to be talking and pointing at you. It's even happening as you drive down the street. Rumors are beginning to circulate around town about you and some of your friends are now involved. As time stretches on into weeks and then months, there seems to be no end in sight of this constant name-calling and finger-pointing.   If you're like most people who've experienced this type of occurrence, your life sucks, right? Well, just image how these people felt:

> Acts 11:25-26 Then departed Barnabas to Tarsus, for to
> seek Saul: (26) And when he had found him, he
> brought him unto Antioch. And it came to pass, that a

whole year they assembled themselves with the church, and taught much people. **And the disciples were called Christians first in Antioch.**

Many people think when Jesus rose on the third day that He went about the business of creating a global religious network which trademarked the name of Christian, and created a whole series of special-needs programs which could only be used in the franchised operations He organized.

They further think that, due to the popularity of this new franchise industry, other people began their own community center modeled after Him and began delivering a similar product, but maybe they changed the ingredients in the "special sauce" or emphasized more of one program versus another so they wouldn't be in violation of the trademark agreement Jesus set up with the Roman government.

However, show them this verse in Acts 11 and explain that it really was, in Hebrew, the "Goyim" - or in today's vernacular, the heathen scum who didn't know any better - who made the brilliant assessment and associated the disciples with the Lord Jesus.

Yes, the term Christian doesn't come from the community called "church," it comes from the people who are watching what's going on in the church. This means something must have been happening which set them apart in order to create a new name to match the association. How did we get from "Christian" to "church?"

So smitten were the disciples with this term that they went right out and stuck it right onto the front of every church they had: The First Church of Ephesus, The First Church of Symrna, The First Church of Pergamos, The First Church of Thyatira, and so on. All right maybe not at first but soon they did - we just don't know when. But we can be assured that even if the disciples didn't do it first, the heathen did, and they had a reason to do so. They saw something different which made the disciples stand out. Can the same be said for you? (Not that you stick names on things, but that you stand out.)

Every group has a code or rite of passage that makes the members of the group associated with each other. I remember as I was growing up if you wanted to hang around with me and my friends you had to be able to hide in the bushes when girls came along so they would see how incredibly dull we were. (We didn't have many members.)

Christians are no different. They have elevated to an art form what goes beyond the requirements of the Bible in some instances. Case in point, let me ask you something: Are you born again? If so, how do know you are, and of what importance is it? Don't go getting yourself into a lather now. I do have a point here that I wish to make, and these two questions are part of the revelation which is unfolding. So please take a moment to answer my questions.

The next set of questions is: Is there a difference between a person who is born again and one who is saved? Can you be one and not the other? Are those called "Sons of God" born again or saved?

Theologians reading this now are having a field day. I am more than likely being branded a heretic, lunatic or being excommunicated from every denomination that ever existed. Questions do that and left to themselves, those are the results you get. Answers on the other hand bring liberty. So in the words of Harry Callahan, "Are you feeling lucky?" Let's go chew on some liberty.

Born Again

The church has built vast doctrines around the mention of one term which has become celebrated throughout the church and nowhere else in society. That's right, let's all say it together, "Are you born again?" It has become kind of a holy code. Parents are reminded to make sure that anybody who wishes to take their child's hand in marriage be, yes, "born again". If a co-worker is to be invited over to dinner with the family, it must be ascertained whether or not the worker is, yes, "born again". And if a person is lying gravely ill in a bed, the first question we must ask in response to their apparent weakness is, is this person, yes, "born again". Am I going to extremes here? Only to make a point. Let's look at the real meaning behind this phrase and why today it's being taken out of context by far too many well-intended people. We'll find it in John, chapter 3.

> *John 3:1-8 There was a man of the Pharisees, named Nicodemus, a ruler of the Jews: (2) The same came to Jesus by night, and said unto him, Rabbi, we know that thou art a teacher come from God: for no man can do these miracles that thou doest, except God be with him. (3) Jesus answered and said unto him, Verily, verily, I say unto thee,* **Except a man be born again,** *he cannot see the kingdom of God. (4) Nicodemus saith unto him, How can a man be born when he is old? can he enter the second time into his mother's womb, and be born? (5) Jesus answered, Verily, verily, I say unto thee, Except a man be born of water and of the Spirit, he cannot enter into the kingdom of God. (6) That which is born of the flesh is flesh; and that which is born of the Spirit is spirit. (7)* **Marvel not that I said unto thee, Ye must be born again.** *(8) The wind bloweth where it listeth, and thou hearest the sound thereof, but canst not tell whence it cometh, and whither it goeth: so is every one that is born of the Spirit.*

Okay let's break this down with the information you know from what you've read. A.) Nicodemus is important; he is a Pharisee and a ruler of the Jews; b.) He recognizes Jesus as a Rabbi, a teacher with a God inspired message, which is evidenced in the miracles that occur. So what is he looking for? Apparently he wants to know how Jesus is able to do what he can't seem to do on his own, namely the miracles that follow the teaching. But because he is a Pharisee, he can't just come out and say, "Hey, how come I don't get the kind of results that you get when I teach the people?" So Jesus answers the unasked, but implied question with the now illustrious statement, "Except a man be born again..." But wait ... what's this trailing along on the same sentence? "... see the Kingdom of God."

No one told me the reason I had to have my co-workers "born again" was so they could see the Kingdom of God! And Jesus even goes further and says they must be born of water and of the Spirit before they can even enter into the Kingdom of God. So my new daughter-in-law and the accompanying dinner guests will have to be water baptized and Holy Spirit baptized in order to see and enter into the Kingdom of God when they come into my house for dinner. (I don't really have a problem with the water part since I believe that any respectable dinner guest should have a bath before attending a dinner event.) Excuse me for a moment while I marvel about this. (Oh, sorry Jesus said not to do that. But that didn't stop Nicodemus from doing it!) So let's see where Jesus takes Nicodemus from here.

> *John 3:9-17 Nicodemus answered and said unto him, How can these things be? (10) Jesus answered and said unto him, Art thou a master of Israel, and knowest not these things? (11) Verily, verily, I say unto thee, We speak that we do know, and testify that we have seen; and ye receive not our witness. (12) If I have told you earthly things, and ye believe not, how shall ye believe, if I tell you of heavenly things? (13) And no man hath ascended up to heaven, but he that came down from heaven, even the Son of man which is in heaven. (14) And as Moses lifted up the serpent in the wilderness, even so must the Son of man be*

lifted up: (15) That whosoever believeth in him should not perish, but have eternal life. (16) For God so loved the world, that he gave his only begotten Son, that whosoever believeth in him should not perish, but have everlasting life. (17) For God sent not his Son into the world to condemn the world; but that the world through him might be saved.

Well if that don't beat all! Nicodemus was supposed to know what Jesus was talking about. Sure Jesus speaks in riddles sometimes, but when you're a Pharisee or "master of Israel," you're supposed to know the secret code and what it unlocks. (Nicodemus must have been at home sick that day when it was revealed to the rest of the class.) So what happens next? Jesus, realizing that He is speaking to someone who parades himself around as though he knows it all, takes Nicodemus on a lesson in Jewish history which will explain what he is trying to put across in terms that he'll be able to relate to. And to further drive home the point, Jesus then displays the famed stadium billboard "John 3:16" just to emphasize that the whole world is watching this event unfold in front of him, and they're cheering him on. Finally, Jesus releases the bitterest of all pills for Nicodemus to swallow: He doesn't hold anything against him or the rest of his gang - He is only there to help.

So here is the breakdown of being born again:

• A religious ruler of Israel comes to find out why when he teaches the people, he doesn't see miracles like Jesus does.

- Jesus declares the secret of his ministry has to do with the Kingdom of God and what He, Jesus, has had to go through to have it operate in His life.

- Surprised it could be that simple, Nicodemus doesn't realize all that he has been doing in his life is a shadow of what Jesus has described.

- In order to bring clarity to the traditions performed, Jesus explains the significance of baptism, of Moses' action in the wilderness, and how they relate to the miracle of healing.

- Nicodemus finally realizes that the whole world is involved in God's overall plan, but because of the world's lack of knowledge about Jewish history and culture, Jesus reveals the secret code of the Kingdom and what knowing the code accomplishes.

The revelation of being born again for all your future party guests or potential in-laws is that, if you are requiring these people to perform miracles at any time during the festivities, they must be born again, which includes being fully immersed in a tub of water and then in the Spirit of God, since Jesus clearly shows this is the only process which will work since it requires being in the Kingdom of God. Yes, miracles are great achievements, but they aren't something just anyone can accomplish. You have to be tapped into the source, and only the Kingdom of God is the pure source. This requires that you must be a subject of the Kingdom and this only occurs when you are born into it – a process which only happens from water and the Spirit. Now that this is settled, let's ask ...

Are you saved?

Versus 16 and 17 of John 3 are the foundations of our next study.

> *John 3:16-17 For God so loved the world, that he gave his only begotten Son, that whosoever believeth in him should not perish, but have everlasting life. (17) For God sent not his Son into the world to condemn the world; but that the world through him might be saved.*

A few paragraphs ago I jokingly commented about Jesus displaying the stadium billboard to Nicodemus (yes, I was too joking!). For those of you who are reading this, but don't have any idea what I'm talking about, let me explain, even though it will dim the wit and charm I envisioned in the proceeding entry.

For a number of years now a gentleman, zealous for the souls of people in the world, has brazenly displayed a placard with the words "John 3:16" at numerous sporting events. What makes his adventures so intriguing is that he somehow manages to always place himself within the crowd right where the television cameras focus during a critical moment of the game. It has been a very successful run for him and those who have tried to copy his style. But let me ask you something (as I have a tendency to do): Isn't "John 3:16" a code for the church?

You don't think, for a moment, that those "in the world" sincerely recognize this to mean they need to pick up their Bibles, turn to the book of John, the third chapter, and read the sixteenth verse do you? So the dilemma I see is that this sincere man is preaching to the choir.   And worse yet, he is doing it when it's fourth down, game tied and three seconds left on the clock.

Do you think I'm going to find time at that very moment to pick up my Bible and read this passage? Heck, I'm too busy praying that the kicker will hook it so my team will win. (Oh, I'm sorry, that was probably too personal.) Yes, by God! My Bible is in my hand waiting for the moment when this placard will unfurl again before my eyes and I am reminded of my salvation as the ball misses the up-rights!

Back to where I was going with this. Let's look again at what the verses say.

> *John 3:16-17 For God so loved the world, that he gave his only begotten Son, that whosoever believeth in him should not perish, but have everlasting life. (17) For God sent not his Son into the world to condemn the world; but that the world through him might be saved.*

If you've been in "The Way" for any period of time you've heard a number of sermons preached about the significance of this passage. So I'm not going to spend a lot of time here. But there are a few points I want to direct your attention to since it is essential in defining our course through this material.

The first thing we need to look at is your perception of the fall. Do you think God was caught off guard when Adam ate from the tree of the knowledge of good and evil? This is not a trick question. Do you think after they eat, God slapped His forehead and said, "Great! Now what am I going to do with you two?" If you're any kind of Bible scholar, you know "before the foundation of the world" God devised a plan to take into account any stupid, idiotic, sophomoric and downright weird thing that man could possible do which would drive man from His presence. (If this comes as news to you, just sit there and thank Him before you go on.)

So the eternal God wants to spend time with you, a human. Pretty cooool! So how much time do you think He wants to spend with you? You think, what, maybe an hour? A couple of hours? Maybe a whole day? Or how about a whole week? Come on, this is God after all: the one person who knows where you hid the lint in your navel. Maybe you should seriously think about this. A year is good, but is that what He wants? How old are you? Are you 10, 18, 25, or over 40 years old? Let's stretch for a moment and read the text again because the answer is found in the last two words of verse 16.

> *John 3:16 For God so loved the world, that he gave his only begotten Son, that whosoever believeth in him should not perish, but have **everlasting life**.*

Whoa! Wrap your head around this one if you can: everlasting (or eternal) life. Forever, dude! Like after tomorrow and on into who knows where. But hold on, there's more. That word "life" is not any normal kind of life which you've ever experienced. It is in its original Greek translation the word "Zoë." You remember the Greek's? They gave us the Olympics, the minor god, Zeus (and a whole host of mythological characters), Socrates, Plato, baklava, feta cheese and many other thing too numerous to mention. Zoë means life to the Greeks, but it represents the kind of life God has, not the kind humans have. Jesus is saying that God wants to spend all of eternity with you, and in order for you to do so with Him, your life has to match His. This is pretty awesome stuff. You, God, together forever, whoa!

Excuse me. I sometimes get caught up in the shear wonder of all this and just go sideways. Let me try to regroup now. Verse 16 says that if you believe in Jesus, the only begotten Son, you won't be treated like road kill in this world but will have a life with God just like Him. And then verse 17 states:

*John 3:17 For God sent not his Son into the world to condemn the world; but that the world through him might be **saved**.*

Look at the last word in this verse: saved. Remember this is Greek? This word is sozo, which according to the Greeks means to be saved, protected, healed, and made whole. This is a vital word we need to understand due to its implications into the next few chapters. So, in order for me to help you grasp the fullness of this meaning, I need to develop a picture in your mind which will better illuminate what is being described here.

Imagine for a moment that you're sailing in a small boat on the sea. Suddenly another ship comes up alongside of you and the crew boards your vessel. They beat you up and cut you with their knives. Then they throw you over board, steal whatever possessions you have on board and then sink your boat. Leaving you floating helplessly in the sea, blood swirling around the cuts in your body, they sail away. You need sozo now! Yes God reaches down, pulls you out of the water, heals your cuts, returns your stolen property, makes your vessel float again and finally ensures no one will maliciously bother you again. One moment you're drowning, and next you're high and dry with a beautiful tan and the wind blowing in your hair. This is the power of sozo!

So how do you activate this wonderful power, this sozo? I thought you would never ask. Follow me to the book of Romans, chapter 10. Some of you veterans in the faith know where we're headed: yes, the Romans Road. But I don't plan on taking the expressway; we're going over land. This is the purpose to the whole manuscript you hold in your hand. But I digress. Let's start at verse 1 and go to verse 13. As has been my method throughout, I'll break it down afterwards.

*Romans 10:1-13 Brethren, my heart's desire and prayer to God for Israel is, that they might be **saved**. (2)*

*For I bear them record that they have a zeal of God, but not according to knowledge. (3) For they being ignorant of God's righteousness, and going about to establish their own righteousness, have not submitted themselves unto the righteousness of God. (4) For Christ is the end of the law for righteousness to every one that believeth. (5) For Moses describeth the righteousness which is of the law, That the man which doeth those things shall live by them. (6) But the righteousness which is of faith speaketh on this wise, Say not in thine heart, Who shall ascend into heaven? (that is, to bring Christ down from above:) (7) Or, Who shall descend into the deep? (that is, to bring up Christ again from the dead.) (8) But what saith it? The word is nigh thee, even in thy mouth, and in thy heart: that is, the word of faith, which we preach; (9) **That if thou shalt confess with thy mouth the Lord Jesus, and shalt believe in thine heart that God hath raised him from the dead, thou shalt be saved.** (10) For with the heart man believeth unto righteousness; and with the mouth **confession is made unto salvation.** (11) For the scripture saith, Whosoever believeth on him shall not be ashamed. (12) For there is no difference between the Jew and the Greek: for the same Lord over all is rich unto all that call upon him. (13) For whosoever shall call upon the name of the Lord **shall be saved**.*

There is a bunch of material here to cover but I want at this time to just look at the references dealing with our main topic at the moment. I'll try to revisit the rest of the material later. First, the apostle Paul opens up about his desire to have his people saved. The importance in this statement is that Paul acknowledges that there is not one thing he can do to save them. This applies equally to you and me. Salvation only comes from God. It's His bat, His ball, and even His field. So we play by His rules. Next, Paul briefly describes how Israel has missed it in the past (this is what I'll get to latter), and leads up to the secret we've been looking for in verse 9. In order to access the power of sozo there are two things you must do: 1) confess and, 2) believe.

I must confess at this time I don't have a very dear regard for those who don't know anything about what the term "confess" means. That is why I am compelled to tell you right now what it means even if you already know. Following the lessons I've learned from Mrs. Thompson, my old English teacher (I'll reveal more about her ways later), confess means: *to own; to acknowledge; to declare to be true, or to admit or assent to in words; opposed to deny.* So according to verse 9, you confess with your mouth, (just like the definition says, in words, not just a nod of the head!) the Lord Jesus. What!? May I ask for a sidebar for a moment? (not a salad bar, a sidebar: a short news story presenting sidelights on a major story)

> *In our fast paced modern society, many have forgotten that the structures of government have not always been democratic, republic or socialistic in nature. The founding of many nations began as tribal interventions into new territories. As these territories primarily were conquered and subsequently defended by family structures, it became apparent that the heads of these families had to have a title which would designate who was*

to be the head, or master. The recognizable term of "king" followed most of these individuals. Additionally, the term "lord " became popular in describing these same people especially in areas where vast amounts of land were under the possession of the realm of the king. The term "Lord" designated ownership and entitlement, which carried with it the responsibility of providing for the inhabitants of the realm. The extent of this provision was entirely up to the lord of the realm. It could consist of food, shelter, and/or protection from surrounding kingdoms. All members in the kingdom agreed to the terms that were set forth by the lord of the realm if they wished to participate in or enjoin his provision. This matter might have been recognized in a formal ceremony where a covenant agreement would be rendered before all the members in the kingdom. The lord would define his responsibilities, and the populace would declare theirs. An allegiance to any heir who followed the lord, should succession be required, would additionally be defined. All would be bound to this agreement. Now, when foreigners would enter into the land in an attempt to steal, rob, or pillage the people could call out to their lord for the protection he promised to provide. If foreigners came into the land to transact business, the people would direct them to the lord since, their allegiance was to him alone and not to any other kingdom. This leads us back to our previous discussion about what you confess.

So what are you going to confess? The Lord Jesus. Does he own you? If you're not certain about that, don't be too concerned right now. By the time you get finished reading all I'm going to show you throughout this manuscript, you'll know with full assurance whether He owns you or not. You'll then know what you're confessing about.

Now let's talk about the second requirement of verse 9 to receive the sozo power: believe. You may have heard the saying, *"If you don't believe something, you'll believe anything."* Well in our course here, you have a very definite belief, or faith, for something, namely the power which comes from being saved. And yet there is a component in this belief that requires you to accept and believe in a higher thing. It is clearly stated in the second part of verse 9, *"...and shalt believe in thine heart that God hath raised him from the dead, thou shalt be saved."* Resurrection - your belief in it coupled with your confession - is what gives you the sozo power. So here is the question: Do you believe in the miraculous power of the resurrection not only as it applies to Jesus but to you also?

That question may have tweaked a few minds just then. Many believe in the resurrection of Jesus, but as it applies to them, they can't seem to make the connection. It is probably the inability to connect on this level which has caused the enemy to exploit a chink in the armor we think we've so properly attired ourselves in. We must remember that it is the truth you know which sets you free, not what you've been told the truth is supposed to be. You wear a helmet of salvation, a hat of sozo. You had better know that it is on your head for a reason – not just as a fashion statement. Look at the verse which references this:

Ephesians 6:17 And take the helmet of salvation, and the sword of the Spirit, which is the word of God:

Notice that the helmet is associated with the sword, or another way of expressing it is that salvation is associated with the words you speak about God. This sentence is the same as Romans 10:9 except window dressing has been added for those who are fashion minded. A helmet is worn to protect your head from your thought about how indestructible your head is. I'll repeat this in case you missed it: A helmet is worn to protect your head from your thought about how indestructible your head is.

Most of you probably think, *"Wait a minute. My head isn't indestructible! This guy is off his rocker."* The trouble is that it's you thinking – this is not God's thought about you in His helmet. God even says so.

Isaiah 55:8-9 For my thoughts are not your thoughts, neither are your ways my ways, saith the LORD. (9) For as the heavens are higher than the earth, so are my ways higher than your ways, and my thoughts than your thoughts.

"Out of context!!! You're taking that out of context!!!" In case you haven't realized this yet, most of the New Testament references to Old Testament scriptures are taken out of context, and yet that didn't stop them from being canonized. But to make my point, let's ask and answer a couple of questions: 1) Why do people wear a hat? To protect their head from the

elements like sun, wind and/or rain. 2) Why does God, the creator of the universe and all that is in it, need a helmet of salvation to wear? Well of course He doesn't, it's a metaphor. And what's with this protection from the elements? Isn't God referred to as the Sun, the Wind and the Rain in the scriptures? So is He trying to protect Himself from Himself? Give me a break! (I can act just as silly as you can if I so desire.)

Where was I? Uhm ...bath or drown ... Nick at night ... miracles at dinner ... Bible codes at a football games ... rocky road I scream in Romans ... ah yes! Resurrection. I may have said this already but it bares repeating: The thing which saves you is believing in a miracle, and because this miracle was accomplished by the one man named Jesus over two thousand years ago, what happens to you is that you never have to die, unless for some strange, way-out-there-kind-of reason, you really want to. God has had a plan in motion since before the foundations of the world, and He is waiting for us to catch on to it and walk it out. But unless we overcome the deception the enemy has heaped upon us, we'll continue to walk the same walk that has been going on for two thousand years. This walk has already turned into ruts for many people, and all a rut is a grave without the ends.

Let me bring up a point here which might surprise some of you: The difference between being born-again and saved depends entirely upon whom you're speaking to. The end result is the same: seeing the Kingdom of God. Jesus was speaking to one type of person and Paul was speaking to another. Both were trying to get people to the same end as I've already said, but the "church" has grouped both together under one umbrella called salvation. But the rain falls on the just and unjust alike, even under an umbrella. So consider this the next time you ask someone if they are born-again. According to the pattern Jesus established for us, that person should be a regular, church going member. Yup, a member of a church - not someone who doesn't know God.

Now I realize this doesn't make sense according to what you've been taught in church. After all, you know all about God and how He operates; you know all about the issues of communion, faith, love, praise and worship, tithing and offerings, and a whole panorama of rituals that describe the religious life you lead. Sounds just like Nick doesn't it? Jesus was pointing to Nicodemus's personal issues and saying, "Look dude, you're so wrapped up in the system that spawned you and the environment it has created, you just don't have any way of coming into the greatness of God's Kingdom unless you're born into it just like you were with the system you're in. And the only way for that to happen is to allow the Spirit of God to breath on you in a manner you won't be able to detect." Guess what? Jesus is saying the same thing today that He said over two thousand years ago to exactly the same people!

Come on, 'fess up. You're just like Nick, (excuse me, Nicodemus) aren't you? You want to see miracles happen, speak the word with power and authority, be thronged by multitudes of people clamoring to sit at your feet and feed on your every word. You want to do all this while attending your comfortable little church service with the cushioned pews, power-point sermons and grand organ concertos. And yet there is something gnawing within you that says there has to be more to your life than this. Church has got to be more than two services on Sunday, one on Wednesday, prayer service on Thursday, and fish on Friday. Right?

This is what Jesus was trying to tell Nicodemus. But church folks are so calibrated to their past teaching that it just takes too much time to deprogram them and then reprogram them with the correct thinking; it would be best if you were just a kid again. Paul, on the other hand, was talking to people who weren't bound up with all the rituals the Jews faced, so all he said was, "Hey, look buddy, it's simple. If you want to be in the Kingdom of God, all you have to do is believe God raised Jesus from the dead and that He is Lord over everything. Easy, right?" Notice that born again people don't have to believe this simple truth mainly because they have (or should have) been instructed in its purpose throughout their religious life, and believe it or not, it becomes a part of your identity upon rebirth. That is what the exchange with Jesus is all about.

We need to have a fresh revelation on the Kingdom concept of exchange, for without it, we'll never know what Jesus accomplished for us. That is where I'm heading next after a slight detour. So buckle up and hold onto your hat. You're in for a ride. (For those of you keeping track, you're right, I haven't answered all the questions I've raised in this chapter. So hang in there – I'm working on it.)

Oh that wonderful prefix "re".

Language is an interesting subject to study. Many of us use words which have lost there meaning primarily due to the fact that we don't care. After all, who has the time to sit down and research the origin of a word and what the derivatives of it are? We know the words we've been taught in English classes from third to fifth grade and stopped learning any more when it became to labourious too spel. (just joking!)

So how many of you remember what a prefix is? I had an English teacher named Mrs. Thompson who would say, *"A prefix is a letter, syllable or word put to the beginning of a word, usually to vary its signification. A prefix is united with the word, forming a part of it; hence it is distinguished...yada yada yada..."* you get the point. (Little did I know at the time that her entire dialogue with us as a class was merely a reciting of definitions from Webster's dictionary! Brilliantly simple, and effective with the unlearned.)

What is all of this leading up to? Obviously you skipped over the title of the chapter! The prefix "re". All right, it has already been established that you don't have time to study the origin of words let alone the many complex facets that derive from them. So while you take a moment out of your busy day to read this, I'm going to enlighten you about this prefix. If you think you can skip this part I would suggest for a moment that you control your impatient self since every great story requires some background material to keep the interest of the reader. Consider this not mere filler in the plot line of this manuscript but as character development upon which all the material in the story hangs.

Taking a page out of Mrs. Thompson's playbook, the word "re" is a prefix or inseparable particle in the composition of words, denotes return, again, anew, back, repetition, or iteration. The importance of this small prefix comes from the word which it is attached to. Here are a few examples: reborn, restore, restitution, resume, recover, resurrect, reveal, revert, revive, resist, remember, remedy, and a whole bunch I don't wish to go into now. You should note that "re" attached to most words gives the connotation that something is going to start over with the implication that it will do so as at the beginning. This prefix is the Rosetta Stone of the New Testament. Don't tell me you don't know what the Rosetta Stone is. (Those of you who do, please bear with me, since this metaphor is vital to the overwhelming use of the word "re" in the Bible.)

> *According to Wikipedia, "The Rosetta Stone is a Ptolemaic era stele (a pillar) written with the same passage of writing in two Egyptian language scripts (hieroglyphic and demotic) and in classical Greek. It*

> *was created in 196 BC, discovered by the French in 1799 at Rosetta, a harbor on the Mediterranean coast in Egypt, and translated in 1822 by Frenchman Jean-François Champollion. Comparative translations of the stone assisted in understanding many previously undecipherable examples of hieroglyphic writing. The text of the Rosetta Stone is a decree from Ptolemy V, describing the repealing of various taxes and instructions to erect statues in temples."[2]*

The original text for the Bible is written in Hebrew for the Old Testament and Greek for the New Testament. Since the common folk of the world are not very fluent in these written languages, some king in England named James decided to have them translated into English, but it had to be the King's English of all things. (When you're the king you can do as you please. Remember that; it's important later on.)

Now here is where the metaphor ends up. Like the Rosetta Stone, three languages are used in the Bible; two are strange and unknown to most people living these days, and the third can be understood by most and helps to explain the other two.

So back to our revelation on the prefix "re". Since we now recognize its meaning is to go back as at the beginning, we should have a better understanding on what these words mean. In the following chart I have provided a series of words which use "re". I have listed the word and what the original meaning

---

[2] http://en.wikipedia.org/wiki/Rosetta_Stone

of the root is to give us a better understanding of what is at work here.

Word	Original Root	With "re" added
Re-born	To birth	To be born as at the first.
Re-store	Store, story, history	To return as was before
Re-stitution	Store, story, history	To return as was before
Re-concile	To be draw as a council, assembly	To call back to union
Re-cover	To take	To take back to a beginning condition
Re-surrect	To rise	To rise back from dead as at first
Re-veal	To veil	To see as before the veil
Re-vert	To turn	To change back to the beginning
Re-vive	To live	To bring back to the life as before
Re-sist	To stand	To stand as before a fall
Re-member	Memory	To have the mind previous

| Re-medy | To heal | To establish health as at the beginning |
| Re-velation | To veil | To see as before the veil |

Now I understand these definitions are simple enough for most of us to grasp and might in many ways be too simple for the complexities we are about to delve into. But I want it that way for a reason. Jesus said we must have the faith of a child, not a college education. (I haven't even mentioned the prefix "pre" which is even more extreme than "re" because it would demand an entire book just from its potential!)

Again, the point I'm trying to make is that the prefix "re" purports to take us back to a moment just before an event. *"What moment from which event are you talking about?"* you may ask. All things start at ... the Beginning.

Eternal Life.

The first exchange

No one knows when it happened, only how it did. And the result has been a war, long, and costly with no apparent end in site. The most depressing news has been the number of prisoners who have been taken and are being held in some of the worst conditions imaginable. Reports come in daily about how these prisoners are being treated in the enemy's territory; reports of torture and abuse, starvation and deprivation, sickness and disease. The commander of the armed forces, moved with compassion for these people, has taken extraordinary actions and proposed a prisoner exchange. These prisoners will be released from their bonds and shackles and the conditions that have oppressed them for so long with the simple mechanism of an exchange.

On the day of the exchange, the commanders of each force stood opposite each other overlooking the battlefield where the transfer was to take place. For as far as the eye could see, the oppressed were clamoring for safety before tensions broke. An ominous rumbling was rising into the air from the sound of feet shuffling across rugged, rocky soil as they approached the demarcation line. As the noise grew louder to almost deafening proportions, a sudden silence snuffed out every trace of hopelessness expressed in their walk. Sorrowful heads lifted and sore eyes strained to peer through the dust and smoke of a gray battlefield. There before them stood the person who would erase the turmoil they had experienced and catapult them back into the safety of their rightful position. Jesus.

Yes, one Man completed the exchange for everyone. When we examine the meaning of exchange most common is the daily exchange where one person gives another something for something like when I give a quarter for a glass of lemonade, or a kiss on the cheek for a rub on the back. Something of value is given in exchange for equal or comparable value. In the eyes of God, to re-deem mankind, He exchanged His only begotten son for all of humanity. But why? I confess, knowing a little about the nature of mankind, I do not have all the answers for this, yet I will proceed to re-veal what I do have. So let's begin. Let's look at God's original intent for man since this will give us a point of reference from which to evaluate our progress.

> *Gen 1:26-30* **And God said, Let us make man in our image, after our likeness: and let them have dominion** *over the fish of the sea, and over the fowl of the air, and over the cattle, and over all the earth, and over every creeping thing that creepeth upon the earth. (27)* **So God created man in his own image, in the image of God created he him; male and female created he them.** *(28) And God blessed them, and God said unto them, Be fruitful, and multiply, and replenish the earth, and subdue it: and have dominion over the fish of the sea, and over the fowl of the air, and over every living thing that*

moveth upon the earth. (29) And God said, Behold, I have given you every herb bearing seed, which is upon the face of all the earth, and every tree, in the which is the fruit of a tree yielding seed; to you it shall be for meat. (30) And to every beast of the earth, and to every fowl of the air, and to every thing that creepeth upon the earth, wherein there is life, I have given every green herb for meat: and it was so.

God declares that man is to be made in His image and likeness. When you look into a mirror or at your baby photos, you are seeing an image of you. It isn't you since it is flat – there is no form, no dimensional characteristics to re-present your natural body structure. This image is transitory when viewed in the mirror, since when you move it goes with you, yet the photograph will retain its image as long as the medium holding the image remains intact. You've probably experienced this dilemma: You're looking at old photos with a close family member and they quickly jerk a picture away from the stack and hold it up next to you. You watch first in surprise and then with disgust as they scan first the picture and then you, one following the other for an extremely long period of time. Maybe you've even experienced the befuddling mannerism of "Tsk... .tsk ... tsk," every time their eyes centered upon the fullness of your natural frame, or the "whosh," of deflated expectations as they re-turned back to the picture. Well rise up! They are comparing the real you to an image. (Regrettably, the image is what is more memorable over time.) So God makes man in His image so that when the animals and plants of the earth look at man, they re-cognize him to be God.

Gasp! That was God's original intent?! I didn't say so, the Bible did. I know that can be a shock to you especially if you've been told all your religious life that the best you can expect is mud, misery and maggots in the sight of God. Religion has a way of doing that to people, even Jesus experienced it.

> *John 10:32-35 Jesus answered them, Many good works have I showed you from my Father; for which of those works do ye stone me? (33) The Jews answered him, saying, For a good work we stone thee not; but for blasphemy; and because that thou, being a man, makest thyself God. (34)* **Jesus answered them, Is it not written in your law, I said, Ye are gods** *(35) If he called them gods, unto whom the word of God came, and the Scripture cannot be broken; (36) Say ye of him, whom the Father hath sanctified, and sent into the world, Thou blasphemest; because I said, I am the Son of God?*

Jesus is referencing Psalms 82, which is a pretty cool Kingdom scripture that I'm not going to elaborate on - just go read it for yourself to better understand where this is going. The following is what I wrote about this subject in my book, *A Kingdom Primer.*

> The original intent of the Father was that man was to be made in the image and likeness of God. One definition states that likeness is: "the quality or state of being alike." So not only was man to look like God, he was to be like

God. This means the way man acts or operates on earth was to be just like God would. So what was all this for? After all, if you're going to look and act like God, there has to be a purpose, right? The purpose was, and still is, to have dominion over the fish, birds, cattle, earth and creeps. Authority, rulership or lordship, that's God's plan for man. Note how there is not listed in man's dominion the mandate to rule over man, but only those things which had been created by God to support man.

Gen 2:7 And the LORD God formed man of the dust of the ground, and breathed into his nostrils the breath of life; and man became a living soul.

So God takes some dust, moulds and fashions it into a body which looks like Him, and then breaths the eternal breath of the God-kind of life into the nostrils and man became a living soul. Man's first image was his Creator, the lifter of his head. Made in the image and likeness, man looks into the face of the One whom he is most like, and this action of looking, of peering, of seeking, is natural. There is no turning away of the head in false humility; no casting down of the eyes in fear. There is a wonder, an intrigue, a sense of awe at the shear spectacle which surrounds him. This is where man started and was to live. What happened to change it all?

Look, I'm not going to go into everything that happened. You know the party line: God says Adam can't eat from the tree of the knowledge of good and evil or he dies; satan appears as a snake deceives the woman into eating the fruit from the very same tree; Adam is right beside her and partakes too; the man and woman realize they are naked; God comes strolling and "can't find them";

then everyone is blaming everyone else, and finally God has to punish all the players involved starting with the snake, then the woman, and finally the man. I'm going to pick it up here at the punishment edicts. God proclaims the following:

> *Genesis 3:14-16 And the LORD God said unto the serpent, Because thou hast done this, thou art cursed above all cattle, and above every beast of the field; upon thy belly shalt thou go, and dust shalt thou eat all the days of thy life: (15) And I will put enmity between thee and the woman, and between thy seed and her seed; it shall bruise thy head, and thou shalt bruise his heel. (16) Unto the woman he said, I will greatly multiply thy sorrow and thy conception; in sorrow thou shalt bring forth children; and thy desire shall be to thy husband, and he shall rule over thee.*

To begin with, look at the order in which these actors are addressed. This is an important principle in Kingdom thinking. Many would say God goes after the lesser first, but this is not so when your dealing with dominion-minded people. A king will always speak to the person in charge first. Now this statement is going to feel uncomfortable to you for a moment since the first person God speaks to is the snake. *"Do you mean that the snake was the one in charge? God gave dominion to Adam. He's the one in charge!"* This is not how it works in God's Kingdom. [3]

---

[3] mike hillebrecht, *A Kingdom Primer, The Basics of the Kingdom of God,* Charis Academy Publishing, 2012

Let me see if I can demonstrate it this way: Let's say that your parents are going out for a moment and they ask you to watch after a younger sister. One of the things they ask you to do is to give your sister a snack of three cookies an hour after they leave. After they leave, you become preoccupied with playing and neglect to give the cookies to your sister. When your parents return in an hour and a half your sister bemoans she never received her cookies. So tell me, who is in charge in this situation, you or your sister? If you still think that it's you, you still haven't learned this vital principle: authority is only yours until you fail to follow the rules, then it is transferred, even if you don't think so. I realize this example might appear to be a little too simplistic for this matter, yet it does prove the point. Dominion, authority or power were transferred from Adam to the snake when Adam did what the animal said to do.

I've got to stop here for a moment because I can't go on without getting this off my chest. How many of you have ever heard a snake speak? What about a donkey? Then what's up with these people? Are they Dr. Doolittle or something? I know that a purple dinosaur and a big yellow bird can speak, but really, a snake? (How was that for a diatribe? Have you ever thought for a moment there exists the ability for us to be able to communicate with animals something which may have been lost in the fall of mankind and it will be re-stored to us? It's just a thought, or as they say in the Psalms, "Selah.")

So God's first judgment goes to the one in charge, the snake, and He declares that as far as animals go, being road kill would probably be better off (if cars existed back then), and that dust would be its primary diet. Then to confound him, He decrees that the seed of the woman would bruise the head of his seed with the heel of his foot. For those of you who were biologically challenged in science class like I was, women don't have seeds, men do. Figure that one out! God tells the enemy how he's going down and cloaks it in a mystery. Such Kingdom intrigue! Then He tells the woman how she is going to have kids and run after her husband. Finally, God gets to Adam.

> *Genesis 3:17-19 And unto Adam he said, Because thou hast hearkened unto the voice of thy wife, and hast eaten of the tree, of which I commanded thee, saying, Thou shalt not eat of it: cursed is the ground for thy sake; in sorrow shalt thou eat of it all the days of thy life; (18) Thorns also and thistles shall it bring forth to thee; and thou shalt eat the herb of the field; (19) In the sweat of thy face shalt thou eat bread, till thou return unto the ground; for out of it wast thou taken: for* **dust thou art, and unto dust shalt thou return***.*

This, for many over the centuries, has become man's plot in life: Ashes to ashes and dust to dust. If I may paraphrase, God says, "... look numbskull, your little oversight in this matter has caused the ground to be cursed. I didn't do that, you did. So now you've got to deal with it, whether I intended for you to or not. You're the one I left in charge here, and you can't even get that right. Now I've got some unemployed cherub in a bad disguise to deal with. You'll have to make the best you can of it; after all, I said you would die if you ate the fruit, and that is what will happen some day. And when that happens, you're going back to the very matter which I created you from."

Stop!

Here is something that is vital. Don't go racing on through to the next part of this until you fully understand what has just happened here. This is the linch pin to everything that will happen to mankind from this moment forward. All that has ever and could possibly happen to you and all your kinfolk follows this declaration. Your ignorance does not keep it from happening to you. So pay attention here because there are some legal matters of the Kingdom that need to be re-vealed. I'm going to go slowly just to make sure it all becomes clear. If you reach the conclusion before me, then stay with me. We don't want the rest to get lost.

First, who is in charge? Correct, satan is because he tricked Adam into relinquishing his authority and dominion through the single act of disobeying God's command regarding the tree of the knowledge of good and evil. What is the action God takes upon the dominant character? Correct, He curses him and decrees that he shall eat dust all the days of his life. Notice, God, the Creator of the universe, including man and angels, does not step in and say, "Hold on there, Lucifer. You are not made of this earth. You are then unable to have authority in this realm. I'm taking it away from you and giving it back to Adam." Please stop and acknowledge this revelation. Humans, made from the dust of the earth, only have been given authority in the very realm they were created in. Selah.

So let me repeat, what is the action God takes upon the dominant character? He acknowledges that satan has authority and dominion but declares, with such authority, he shall crawl around on his belly and eat dust all the days of his reign. When you think of someone in a position of power you typically don't think of them lording over you from their belly do you? As for myself, I think of them generally in a position where they're taller than I am or sitting on a throne of some sort. That is what Lucifer thought would happen to him, too. But because he took on the persona of an animal of this planet, satan had to deal with the animal's Creator and His instruction of how he is to operate. For those of you who don't believe the Bible speaks about, or even documents anything about evolution, I provide to you the following verse:

> Genesis 3:14 *And the LORD God said unto the serpent, Because thou hast done this, thou art cursed above all cattle, and above every beast of the field; upon thy belly shalt thou go, and dust shalt thou eat all the days of thy life:*

"... *upon thy belly shalt thou go,*" was the decree. If this was to be a curse, why would God state the obvious nature of an object and declare it to be a curse if it was originally called "good"? I proclaim that the original nature of the snake was not to crawl on its belly. Upon those words the snake went from a walking (possibly talking, but I digress) animal to one which only crawls. There it is: evolution has occurred and the Bible clearly talks about it even if it was the only time it happened!

You'll recall when God created man He declared that man was to have dominion over the planet and multiply. That was man's mandate upon the earth as its ruler. Yet man surrendered his authority over to satan, so now his only remaining directive was to multiply. Many don't recognize that satan was also given a mandate in his new capacity as ruler over (beneath) man. It's in the same verse where God says *"... and dust shalt thou eat all the days of thy life."* I realize that that doesn't sound like much of a mandate but it has been powerful throughout all of man's history. How you might ask. The key is in recognizing what God proclaims to Adam in verse 19:

> *Genesis 3:19 In the sweat of thy face shalt thou eat bread, till thou return unto the ground; for out of it wast thou taken: **for dust thou art, and unto dust shalt thou return.***

Okay, let's land these flights of fancy. In verse 14, God says that satan shall eat the dust of the ground, and then in verse 19 God says Adam shall re-turn to the dust of the ground. There it is. God gave satan authority to eat, chew, devour, consume and destroy Adam and his kin. Selah. I'm not stretching to make a connection between these two verses since they follow one another. Many just have not had this connection revealed to them until now. God gave satan the authority to devour the humans.

The remedy

Are you shocked? Maybe you're miffed. How about a little peeved? What? Is stronger language required? Appalled! Stunned! Mad as hell! Well before you get too bent out of shape look at this:

> *John 10:10 The thief cometh not, but for to steal, and to kill, and to destroy: I am come that they might have life, and that they might have it more abundantly.*

Jesus clearly explains what I just re-vealed to you from the beginning of mankind. Up until Jesus came, satan has had legal authority to eat away at man. All the disease that has been affecting mankind has been because of this devouring mandate. All the pestilence and famine which has inflicted generations is due to this same mandate. It has affected everything that came from the dust of the earth since time began. Was that God's original intention? Despite what some religious sects may tell you, the answer is unequivocally, NO!!! If you have any doubt still about this fact, please go back to the beginning of this chapter and read it again. I'll wait.

You back? Good. Let's take a moment to re-cap for those who didn't have to go back and re-read this chapter. If you don't mind (as if you had a choice!) I'm going to paraphrase this section from the perspective of the antagonist, satan.

"Okay, I'm really bummed.   I've been thrown out of my homeland for thinking about what it would be like to have praises lifted up to me. I'm stuck here on this piece of rock in the middle of nowhere with a bunch of washed up angels. My Creator, the one who tossed me out like some piece of garbage, decides that He is going to remodel my new abode. I don't really have much say in what it's to look like, what colors appeal to my tastes and the overall décor. He just comes by and, in a few days, the whole joint is looking just like where He threw me out of. Great! To add insult to injury, He creates something that I've never seen right out of the very gunk I have to stand in and decides to make it, not me, but IT, the overseer of this forsaken rock. And now to make matters worse, there are two of them.

"Well, I'm not going to stand for this. I'll get rid of them and make myself the top dog of this place. But wait, this could get ugly if I don't do this correctly since they do have a right to be the head of this place, having been crafted here. I know! I'll get them to think. That's what I did and look where it got me. I'll have them think about where I came from and how they don't fit in there and then they'll try to get there. That is sure to upset a few apple carts. Wait a minute. I better try this out on the second one first. It wasn't there when the Creator assigned them their responsibilities, so I'll try this one first just in case I have to go to the other one. That should give me the chance to work out any kinks if things don't go quite right. That's what I'll do. I'll walk over there and ... Oh yeah! I can't walk up to it like this. It would recognize me right off. I need a disguise. But what? There has to be something around here that is as smart and cunning as me. AH yes. The snake.

"Boy, that was easier than I thought. They took it hook, line and sinker. Sure there was some backlash, but that is to be expected when you're dealing with such important matters; it will all wash out in the end. What's important is that I'm in charge now, as it should have always been. I wasn't quite expecting the dust diet but that's okay, I'll still be in control. Sure I'll have to get used to looking up at all I control, but this is a small sacrifice to pay. The man – oh did he get it – I'll never forget the expression on his face when he heard the Creator's voice. Priceless! And the woman was so gullible. Like, "Hello. Anyone home?" There is the matter of her seed though. What was that all about? Bruise my forehead with his heel. I wonder what that means ... her seed ... my seed ... bruising ... heel. What difference does it make now? I'm in charge here. Man, am I hungry after all that. MAN. Did you hear me? I'm hungry. Don't make me slither over to you. Feed Me!"

The topic of this chapter is about the exchange. I've led you up to this point because you need to recognize the value of the first of many exchanges Jesus made. This one is by far the most important of all because your salvation depends on it being made. That is right. Your very salvation is based on this one exchange, and without knowing about the history of how it occurred, its effects and potential of neglect, you walk in a form of godliness but deny its power. You've probably heard about the other exchanges Jesus made for us: being made sin; becoming poor; becoming the sacrificial lamb; taking our stripes and many more that I don't have space to elaborate on. Yet this one, as I've stated is the first and holds all we need to release us from the bondage the enemy has placed upon and about us. As Jesus said in the book of John:

*John 8:31-32   Then said Jesus to those Jews which believed on him, If ye continue in my word, then are ye my disciples indeed; (32) And ye shall know the truth, and **the truth shall make you free**.*

Over the course of some four thousand years, mankind had been held under the sway of a demoted cherub who consistently devoured the very life from the entire creation of God. As hopeless as it may have appeared at times, there was nonetheless a plan in the works operating under the radar of human perception. In the fullness of time, a Redeemer would come upon the scene and, with perfect understanding and knowledge, pay the outstanding demand for the entire realm to be re-stored back to the original intent of the Creator.

We are well aware of the birth, life and ministry of Jesus. So let's cut to the chase and go right to the vital moment. Three and a half years of ministry time have passed for Jesus and his disciples. Miracles, healings, command of the elements and demonic realm have been the hallmark of this time and training. And yet despite all of this, it was merely leading up to these final days of Jesus upon the face of the earth. The knowledge of the events that were about to transpire ran through His mind with increasing ferocity as the minutes passed by the night prior to a climactic Passover ceremony. If only He could talk to His Father then maybe this could be averted somehow.

Luke 22:39-44 And he came out, and went, as he was wont, to the mount of Olives; and his disciples also followed him. (40) And when he was at the place, he said unto them, Pray that ye enter not into temptation. (41) And he was withdrawn from them about a stone's cast, and kneeled down, and prayed, (42) Saying, Father, if thou be willing, remove this cup from me: nevertheless not my will, but thine, be done. (43) And there appeared an angel unto him from heaven, strengthening him. (44) And being in an agony he prayed more earnestly: and his sweat was as it were great drops of blood falling down to the ground.

There is Jesus, in the garden, just like Adam at the beginning, speaking to the Father about the temptation of doing His own will versus the will of the Father. "But Jesus is God. His will and God's will are the same." Hold on there pardner. That hissing you hear is the sound of religion speaking. Yes, Jesus is God, but in this matter, as was all His time on Earth, He is man. John tells us God cannot be tempted, right? So why would Jesus, as God, be speaking to the Father about being tempted if, as God, Jesus, couldn't be tempted?

Man can be tempted, and the scriptures say Jesus endured all the temptations common to man. This one right here is the biggest one and, like the first Adam, was the cause for the whole downfall of mankind. At this precise moment Jesus had to decide whether what He wanted as a man was more important than what God was requiring of him. As a man, he had to submit either to the mission of the Kingdom, which he had been preaching about, or do it his way. The choice was purely his as a man, God's way or his way, freewill or God's will. The hissing you now hear is the sound of hot air being expelled from that religious cow we just cut open.

So let us continue, because there is freedom waiting around the corner. After Jesus prays, an angel comes and strengthens Him while he continues to pray. And look at the last half of verse 44, *"... and his sweat was as it were great drops of blood falling down to the ground."* Blood hits the ground. Pure, spotless, sinless, blood hits the dust just as sweat hit the dust. Adam's judgment in Genesis 3:19 is paid in full with that precious blood. The dust no longer can be eaten by the enemy. The garden has been redeemed, too. Starvation is the only thing available to the enemy of mankind through Jesus.

What makes this act so vital is that it had to happen here first, in a garden, dealing with temptation, just as it happened in the beginning. Only here could the legal aspects of the transfer of dominion be maintained. The Kingdom requires it that way, like for like. This one exchange opened the door to your salvation because no longer could the earth hold onto a human being in death until they returned to dust. The creation, which had to submit itself to the enemy just as man had to, clearly recognizes the legal parameters establishing a true son of God. It knows it cannot hold onto anyone walking as a son of God now that the ransom price of blood has been paid in full. Dust to dust theology went out the door with this exchange but only if you understand it. Ignorance of this matter has kept far too many of the saints in a position of bondage to a master who has not had any authority for over 2,000 years!

*Romans 6:23 For the wages of sin is death; **but the gift of God is eternal life** through Jesus Christ our Lord.*

According to Romans 10:9, your salvation is based on the belief that Jesus was raised from the dead in three days. He was able to accomplish this because the dust was re-deemed from the curse which had been placed upon it from the acts that transpired in the garden at Eden. That re-demption had to abate the power of destruction found in placing a body in the ground and renders as useless the ability of an enemy who feeds on that process.   If this one step on the road to re-storation had not been accomplished first, there could have been no re-surrection. Every other instance where Jesus shed His blood was in part to re-store those attributes true sons of God possess which had been forfeited in the garden. And, since Adam, created from the dust of the earth, began his rule in a garden, Jesus had to bring the realm back into alignment to the original design.

Let's take a moment here to look at a statement Jesus made to Martha as her brother Lazarus slept the day away.

John 11:25-27 Jesus said unto her, I am the resurrection, and the life: he that believeth in me, though he were dead, yet shall he live: (26) And whosoever liveth and believeth in me shall never die. Believest thou this? (27) She saith unto him, Yea, Lord: I believe

---

that thou art the Christ, the Son of God, which should come into the world.

"I am the resurrection, and the life." Maybe Jesus is just boasting here to make Martha focus on something other than her grief. But, if you follow along for a bit, you'll see that Martha has some re-collection of whom Jesus is, and His declaration could hold up according to the traditions Martha and her people had been taught throughout the centuries. Notice how she associates re-surrection and life with the title of the Christ or Messiah. She is so consumed in her grief here that she is re-verting to the doctrine which had established the identity of a people - not to her own values. Yet Jesus didn't ask her about the value of her doctrine. He wanted to know if she valued Him.

When I ask you to believe what I'm saying, I want to determine if you value me, since if you take the words I speak and acknowledge whatever you're hearing as being purposeful to your life, a value is established. The depth of that value can only be determined by the impact the message has on your circumstances. Martha appears more concerned about what her future will be than who is before her at the moment. After all, He hadn't died yet, so how can this claim be valid?

Well, let's take a moment to see what Jesus was making reference to. I'm going to have to go ahead into the future a bit and call on Paul to reveal to us the mystery both Jesus and

Martha were referring to, each in their own unique perspective. Let's start in Galatians 3.

> *Galatians 3:16-19 Now to Abraham and his seed were the promises made. He saith not, And to seeds, as of many; but as of one,* **And to thy seed, which is Christ.** *(17) And this I say, that the covenant, that was confirmed before of God in Christ, the law, which was four hundred and thirty years after, cannot disannul, that it should make the promise of none effect. (18) For if the inheritance be of the law, it is no more of promise: but God gave it to Abraham by promise. (19) Wherefore then serveth the law? It was added because of transgressions,* **till the seed should come to whom the promise was made***; and it was ordained by angels in the hand of a mediator.*

This passage gives us a brief glimpse into Martha's mind (the entire chapter would better illuminate her thoughts yet for brevity I'm going to remain here). The entirety of Jewish thought revolves around Abraham. Here we see the mechanics of what occurred as God promised Abraham that he would be the father of many nations. God's covenant was made with Abram, who then became know as Abraham (the "H" indicating his partnership with the Lord Jehovah). If you are unfamiliar with covenant procedure, I'm going to provide a sidebar in this matter and for those of you who understand it, use this time to either re-fresh your memory or go and get something to drink.

> *A covenant, defined in a ceremony, brings two or more parties together to form an alliance in order*

to continue with a plan or purpose. The most common rendition of this transaction today is a wedding. As such, much of what happens in a wedding best describes what transpires in a covenant ceremony. The parties come together; tokens or gifts are exchanged; these become the identifying markers of their new union; an exchange of drink, often wine, representing the blood, is made between the parties signifying that they now share this in common; bread is also exchanged as a symbol of their long-term care for each other; and both recite a pledge or vow of what will be their responsibilities to each other. The reciting of this pledge is witnessed by others as a reminder to the parties that if one should fail to enforce their responsibility to the compact, then any of the witnesses have full authority to exact justice upon the negligent party. Additionally, there is a person at this ceremony who acts as the mediator between the parties. The mediator is responsible to see that each party brings the appropriate elements to the meeting to address the requirements that are being established in the union. Upon completion of the ceremony, each person takes on the name of the other in some fashion to indicate the union has been made. This also becomes the name of legal recognition in any dispute with other outside parties. Each party is presented to the witnesses at the event now as two having become one. Okay that is your brief lesson on covenant; let's return to our matter at hand.

In Galatians 3:16-19, Paul is describing the covenant ceremony between Abram and God. (If you need further background on this, go to Genesis 12 and keep reading until you're satisfied.) So the Seed we're speaking of here, as Paul

---

reveals, is the Christ or Messiah. Now an important aspect of this ceremony is further described in Hebrews.

> *Hebrews 11:17-18   By faith Abraham, when he was tried, offered up Isaac: and he that had received the promises offered up his only begotten son, (18) Of whom it was said, That in Isaac shall thy seed be called:*

This passage speaks of the trial of Abraham in the offering of his son. Notice, it is not an account of Abram but of Abraham. So we know the covenant with Jehovah has been created and is in operation. Now notice at this trial Abraham had already received his promises from Jehovah (pay attention to the language because this is legal) that in, or through, Isaac shall Abraham's seed be called. I want to clarify this point: Isaac is not the Seed – the Seed comes through him. Isaac is the fruit of the covenant between Abram and Jehovah. So in the book of Galatians we see that the promises God makes are to the Seed, Christ. We also see in verse 19 of Galatians there is a mediator to the parties in the agreement. But look at verse 20.

> *Galatians 3:20 Now a mediator is not a mediator of one, but God is one.*

A mediator works with two parties. God and the Seed of Abraham are the parties, correct? (This is where you respond, "Yes.") Verse 20 merely states the obvious fact that God is one – there are not multiple gods. Yet what is important here in the verse is the knowledge that the Seed, the Christ, and God are one held together in union by the promise which was made by God and mediated by Abraham. So what was the focal promise given? For that we go back to Hebrews 11 and look at the trial again with the last aspect provided.

Hebrews 11:17-19   By faith Abraham, when he was tried, offered up Isaac: and he that had received the promises offered up his only begotten son, (18) Of whom it was said, That in Isaac shall thy seed be called: (19) Accounting that God was able to raise him up, even from the dead; **from whence also he received him in a figure.**

Abraham knowing the promises which God had made to him regarding the Seed, confidently went up to the mountain with the image in his head of Isaac being re-surrected if he should have to kill him. He knew this because he mediated a covenant between two parties, and his responsibility in that position was to oversee that each party fulfilled its obligation. If Isaac died before passing his Seed on, God would be required, no matter what, to bring Isaac back to life: the Seed only comes through him.

So, imparted into Isaac's DNA from Abraham is the promise of a re-surrected life. He may never have known this, but Abraham and God did because Isaac is the fruit of their covenant. So generation after generation this DNA marker traveled down the gene pool until it came to the Recipient of the promise and connected with the corresponding DNA marker of the divine life. "I am the resurrection and the life," is not a statement of some way-out-there event. It was a declaration emanating from a cellular identity which only the Seed of a covenant could proclaim.

So if Christ is the Seed of the promise, when He becomes planted and eventually produces fruit, what will be the characteristics of that fruit? Re-surrection and divine life are hardwired into the DNA. The Seed always produces after its own. Who is the fruit?

Do you believe you are? You do? Good. So which are you: dead or alive? Either way, eternal life is ...

All matter has ears ... and a memory

In this chapter I'm going to try something different. I'm not going to use the actual text from the Bible to illuminate and validate the script. Now this may led some of you to think that error will creep in, and I may stray from the truth of the Word. Would you please sit on your head!

I apologize for my outburst. Many are too quick to pass things off when they go against their past learning styles. What I want to reveal in this section is a little known fact about all teaching: It's already been said. Yes, every subject which has ever been taught and will be taught has already been spoken. So where were you on that day when the subject was taught?

Recall, if you will, a special night. You're sitting with Jesus eating supper and as the meal progresses, He tells you He is about to leave. Many of those around you are disappointed but Jesus tells all of you not to be concerned because He is going to send a comforter, the Holy Spirit, who will "teach you of things to come" and "bring to re-membrance" the teaching that Jesus has given you when you are placed before important people. Now for some reason this statement doesn't seem to make any sense to you, but most of what Jesus said did not make a whole lot of sense at the time. He even would rub it in sometimes by saying, "Whoever has ear to hear, let him hear." Now granted, unlike a few people who came to see Jesus to have their ears opened, you have a perfectly fine set and can hear just dandy. Guess what? Everything has ears. Selah.

Standing on the precipice of eternity, God looks out into the vastness of nothing with a design which He is about to bring into manifestation. Like every artist in the flow of creative expression there comes a declaration of beginning to establish a context for the very act of creation. The first thing, the first action, the first thought, the first enunciation defines the path that is to weave through the messiness which is to follow. Poised in anticipation is the Holy Spirit, like a catcher at the plate waiting for the pitcher to deliver the final throw when the bases are loaded, there's a full count, and the score is tied in the bottom of the ninth.

Since there is no measurement of time in eternity we don't know how long God stood there. Having observed some very talented artists during the creation process, I believe that it seemed like it took all of eternity for Him to eventually do something. Finally, a declaration is heralded from within the very essence of all that ever was, is, and will be. A wave undulates out into nothing with a predetermined pattern of occurrence, wafting forward with constant radial magnitude and amplification. Onward and onward this first wave travels unaware of the subsequent waves following it, each unique in its form and function, all independent but cohesive in their mission. "Light be," resonates throughout the vast nothingness, onward and onward.

I have a teenager who is the spitting image of God. He has to have the light on in every room he enters regardless of the time of day. Mind you, I never have to tell him to turn it on, it is a part of his character, which he has graced me with since he has been able to reach the switch.

So let me ask a question: If the first action determines the foundational attributes of all matter, when a voice is spoken, it is done for what purpose? To hear, obviously. (I'm re-minded of a favorite childhood expression I was privy to: "I'm not talking just to hear myself, young man." I think that saying is revelation straight from the throne room of God!) But many overlook the reality that a voice is an articulation of a thought which came first. That thought was God's foundational act for the voice that followed. The entirety of the thought, its fullness, and its completeness became evident in the voice of its expression. What then was the thought? I'm not totally certain, but I can offer one belief according to Revelation 13:8 - there was a Lamb slain before the foundation of the world.

That act and all of its eternal purposes had to be resonating throughout the entire eternal realm. Every action which subsequently came after this act would be an extension of its purpose. When a voice came forth, it would express the intention behind the action, it would communicate the emotions, thoughts and feelings about the purpose of the event which had preceded its articulation. Because God is all in all, His very words contain the fullness of His nature; there will be nothing lacking when He speaks.

So ears, or some type of receptor, must exist so that the voice waves can be channeled and eventually processed. Yet we know that when the first declaration of God's plan was articulated, there was darkness on the formless void of the deep, and yet the expressed outcome was instantly achieved. So let's break down some basic properties here in order to go deeper into this study. To do that I'm going to write this as a programmer would so you could follow the logic of it.

```
100 God speaks
120 if ears not exist goto 125 else goto 130
125 create ear goto 130
130 evaluate
131 if not authority goto end
132 if not living goto 150
133 if blessing goto 145
134 if curse goto 150
135 if question goto end
136 if joke goto hysterical
140 perform
141 goto end
145 multiply_all
146 goto end
150 perform_and_kill_it
End.
```

I realize this might not be a very complex program but there is beauty in its simplicity. All avenues were thought of in the divine order of things. Notice the creative nature of the word of God when it is released. It has to find a receptor to enter into. If it can't find one, it will create one. God tells us His word will not come back to Him void, meaning it will not travel through a void - it will create a receptor. Think of God's Word as a spiritual cocklebur, traveling through the environment seeking what it may grab onto and, if it can't find anything to attach itself to, it creates that thing.

Once the voice is received, the ear has to determine if it's really God's Word. We've all experienced this process. Mom says repeatedly to pick up your room, and you full, of juvenile exuberance and energy, tone her out. Dad arrives on the scene and states singularly that the room will be picked up. What occurs next is the evaluation of authority and whether you'll live through the result of ignoring this command. Room cleaned.

Life and death are in the power of the tongue and this, too, is an evaluation which must occur after the authority is determined. This matter wasn't truly required when God spoke since He is life, yet knowing that there could be a potential of this occurring, He brilliantly included it within the design. Then there is the matter of blessings and curses which would need to be addressed within the design.

As you can see all which pertains to life was included within the very Word that God spoke. This same program is still running today in all we are surrounded by. When God spoke in Genesis, all matter which was present heard His Word and ran the Word through its ears before accomplishing what was commanded. Now, since God is a spirit, we can assume that all matter has spiritual ears which are tuned to hear the exact frequency of the voice of the Father. This was demonstrated by Jesus many times: He spoke the Word and quieted a storm; He spoke the Word and the servant of the centurion was healed; a man with a withered hand was healed by the command He issued; He taught Peter how to fish for gold; and of course, raised Lazarus from the grave with the Word.

Now many say Jesus could do this because He is God. You're only half right and unfortunately, being half right isn't right at all. John says that Jesus grew in wisdom and stature with God and man. If He was God, how could this verse be true? Jesus was a man on this earth demonstrating the inherent power of the Kingdom of God. What He did is the example of what we can do, too. If He can talk to storms, so can we. If He can heal with a word, so can we. If He can call the dead from out of the grave so can we. We merely need to recognize that all matter has ears which are designed to recognize the voice of God.

In Romans, Paul states that all of creation eagerly awaits the manifestation of the sons of God because it recognizes that these sons will release the creation from the bonds of corruption and death it has been subjected to since the fall occurred. Walking in the divine nature of Christ enables us to release the life-creating nature which the Father and Jesus share.

This is not a blab-it-and-grab-it message. This is a message which answers that all important question: If a tree fell in the forest and no one was around to hear it, does it make a sound? The answer is yes, yes, yes. And everything around it heard it, but since it did not have the same frequency of the Word of God, it didn't create anything when it hit the ground except a loud mess.

The memory of it all

As I mentioned a few moments ago, the creation is eagerly awaiting the sons of God to release it from its bondage. This brings up a curious thought if you're so inclined: Can matter re-member? Haven't you ever wondered where the phrase, "What's the matter; don't you re-member?" came from? Now to some of you (you know who you are so I'm not going to point you out) might think this subject to be so far out in the left-field of practical doctrine that it's not worth discussing. That's okay, you have an opinion which will keep you away from the power of God then. I know you'll be happy in your ignorance. I on the other hand am determined to see the fullness of the Kingdom released in my life and this is a part which needs further insight.

How many of you have records? You know vinyl? Well, all right, how about 8 tracks? Cassettes? Come one you're a church person, you have to have cassettes. Oh you're a new convert. So then you have CD's? Or mp3's? Good, finally a common ground to explain this. Tell me, with any of these items that you have listened to, has there been a difference with the performance from the first time that you heard it until now? (I understand the inherit problem of you in the LP crowd, I possess 200 myself.) So it would be safe for me to say there really isn't much difference between what you're hearing now from what you originally heard. Guess what this is called: memory. Sure it's easy to pass this phenomenon off on technology, but this has been going on for centuries, even millennium. The carbon matter which makes up your computer or CD's all has memory capabilities. Even every day common items have memory.

You may recall me writing earlier about your mother asking you to clean your room. If you were like me, the best excuse to use which has been handed down from generation to generation is, "I forgot." This simple lack of memory would often provide the reprieve which was needed to get the extra time necessary to accomplish the chore that you where required to complete. But let's be honest; we never forgot. We heard the first, and every subsequent time thereafter. It was lodged in our memory, just not in our physique. But the thing that lodged it in our memory was the hearing. After all, if you have ears, you've got to do something with what you hear. Memory is the by-product of hearing. Since I established from the previous section that all matter has ears, it would be safe to consider that all matter also has memory.

The Earth can only be waiting for the sons of God because it has a memory of what a son of God looks like and can recognize one based on memory. Joshua declared that a pile of stones taken from the Jordan River would be a witness to the events which transpired upon the crossing over of the children of Israel into the Promised Land. This is but one of the instances where an object was declared to have a memory of an event in this Earth.

Probably the most important event ever recorded in the Bible of any matter having memory occurred at the crucifixion. Merely hours beforehand, the cleansing action brought on by spilt blood untainted with sin, had begun rippling throughout all of creation, first in a garden and spreading out in undulating fashion across the entire depth and breadth of the planet. Culminating in a crescendo as Jesus expels his last breath declaring the finish, the Earth acknowledging the divine nature which resides within Him, shakes and trembles at the realization that the Creator, the Author of light, will have to dwell within its very shadows. For the first time in all of creation no "ashes to ashes and dust to dust" will follow this man into the darkness, and the earth erupts in joyous celebration by extent of releasing the sleeping saints from previous generations. The divine order has been re-established and a fresh memory has been minted within the creation.

Now, some of you may well say this is merely poetic ramblings of a suspect nature. I will permit you at this moment to hold onto these precarious thoughts, but I will ask you in the same regard to establish a better answer for these areas I've spoken about. The mere existence of an Ipod defines my explanation of matter having memory. I ask you to consider the fullest realization of this concept: The very pages you are reading this from contain memory of all events which have occurred to them from their birth to their present form and, if they had a way of transcribing this information into a form that we all could recognize, they would provide a history lesson which might astound you. Think of the history that is stored within the very walls of the room you're in; the people, the conversations, and the actions which have been recorded within the walls waiting for the day when it can be released. That old spy adage "The walls have ears," is more truth than we want to believe.

Where is all of this taking us? Back to the future, of course. Just as it says in Romans, all the creation is waiting to be released from the bondage Adam subjected it to through his disobedience. Only the sons of God can complete this mission. Yet we need to understand the original design and intent of the Father if we are to release the power that works within us to complete the destiny that has been prepared for us. While we may believe we walk with all authority from our Father in Heaven, the creation will testify to our true level of authority. The spiritual ears which have been created within everything hear everything that is spoken by you, and, following the principles I defined earlier, will determine if your voice is the voice of God on earth. If it is, it will respond with the appropriate actions. If it's not, even if you think it is, it will do what is supposed to do when an interloper comes around.

Think back for a moment on the previous discussion on salvation. The two-part activation required you to believe in re-surrection and confess the Lordship of Jesus. Confession is a spiritual proclamation that resonates in the ears of all creation. It knows the Lord, and it acknowledges His authority over this realm. Your pronouncement is a confirmation of what it has already validated. Yet it provides identification as to the nature which now resides within you that the creation can recognize and work with.

So, we need to acknowledge:

- An ear was present to hear in order to process the command and achieve the desired result.

- This voice creates in its very expression.

- The pattern - voice, hearing and sight

- There is a memory that is recognized throughout all creation.

- Memory validates hearing.

A generation as a witness

Matthew 27:50-54 Jesus, when he had cried again with a loud voice, yielded up the ghost. (51) And, behold, the veil of the temple was rent in twain from the top to the bottom; and the earth did quake, and the rocks rent; **(52) And the graves were opened; and many bodies of the saints which slept arose, (53) And came out of the graves after his resurrection, and went into the holy city, and appeared unto many.** *(54) Now when the centurion, and they that were with him, watching Jesus, saw the earthquake, and those things that were done, they feared greatly, saying, Truly this was the Son of God.*

1 Corinthians 15:52-58 **In a moment, in the twinkling of an eye, at the last trump: for the trumpet shall sound, and the dead shall be raised incorruptible, and we shall be changed.** *(53) For this corruptible must put on incorruption, and this mortal must put on immortality. (54) So when this corruptible shall have put on incorruption, and this mortal shall have put on immortality, then shall be brought to pass the saying that is written, Death is swallowed up in victory. (55) O death, where is thy sting? O grave, where is thy victory? (56) The sting of death is sin; and the strength of sin is the law. (57) But thanks be to God, which giveth us the victory through our Lord Jesus Christ. (58) Therefore, my beloved brethren, be ye stedfast, unmoveable, always abounding in the* *work of the Lord, forasmuch as ye know that your labour is not in vain in the Lord.*

1 Thessalonians 4:13-17 But I would not have you to be ignorant, brethren, concerning them which are asleep, that ye sorrow not, even as others which have no hope. (14) For if we believe that Jesus died and rose again, even so them also which sleep in Jesus will God bring with him. (15) For this we say unto you by the word of the Lord, that we which are alive and remain unto the coming of the Lord shall not prevent them which are asleep. (16) For the Lord himself shall descend from heaven with a shout, with the voice of the archangel, and with the trump of God: and the dead in Christ shall rise first: **(17) Then we which are alive and remain shall be caught up together with them in the clouds, to meet the Lord in the air: and so shall we ever be with the Lord.**

There is a generation who will live and not die. How old will these people be? All of various ages: new-born babies to elderly. But the term elderly is too vague for our purposes here, so let's determine what is generation is. According to Webster's dictionary it is defined as:

> **GENERA'TION**, *n. The act of begetting; procreation, as of animals.*
>
> *1. Production; formation; as the generation of sounds or of curves or equations.*
>
> *2. A single succession in natural descent, as the children of the same parents; hence, an age. Thus*

we say, the third, the fourth, or the tenth generation.

3. The people of the same period, or living at the same time.

4. Genealogy; a series of children or descendants from the same stock.

5. A family; a race.

6. Progeny; offspring.

To summarize this, let's say that a generation is a group who witnesses the birth of an event and, living with the outcome of the event, sees the transition to its final conclusion. Enoch was the seventh generation from the creation of man. Yet he is also the first generation of those who will live and not die, and since the final outcome of this generation has not been completed, we are still in that first generation time frame. So returning back to the age of those declared elderly, it is possible someone in their 70's by today's standards could be "elderly", but still be a babe according to the age of Enoch. Why is this numbering important? We define our existence by the passing of the years we have celebrated. Certain rites of passage are defined by age, or maturity. We establish our successful accomplishments by completing them by a certain age and then expect to receive the rewards of relaxation from a hard-fought life at a certain age. Ultimately, there is the expectation of a heavenly reward again defined by a passage of time defined by years.

Yet Enoch did not die. Why do you want to? You may say, "I don't want to," or, "I don't have a choice," or, "I've worked hard all my life for the Lord and I deserve heaven as my reward!" So lets deal with these responses.

The Great Escape

Most people will remember the movie called "The Great Escape." It tells the story of a prisoner-of-war camp run by the Germans during the Second World War. The premise of the movie is based on how this camp, which had claimed to have no escaped prisoners, deals with a great number of the prisoners, who over the course of many months of planning, perform a "great" escape. Many church-going members view life as living out this movie. They dread the daily monotony which comes with being called Captives for Christ. They eagerly speak in cloaked voices about the plan of the rapture and wait for their great escape from this world into the heavenly realm. Plain and simple: they want out of the daily struggle and into the heavenly realm where they'll lay on clouds all day eating grapes picked by little rotund angels. (Okay I'm embellishing it a bit. But this is the vision that Hollywood has created, right?)

So what are they escaping from? Why Earth of course. It has far too many problems, and to be away from it is to let someone else deal with it. Heaven is where we're supposed to be, that's why Jesus died for us, so we could go to Heaven and live with the Father. Excuse me for a moment. Let's read something so we can get a true heavenly picture of what's going to happen in the final days.

> *Revelation 21:1-4 And I saw a new heaven and a new earth: for the first heaven and the first earth were passed away; and there was no more sea. (2)* **And I John saw the holy city, new Jerusalem, coming down from God out of heaven,** *prepared as a bride adorned for her husband. (3) And I heard a great voice out of heaven saying, Behold, the tabernacle of God is with men, and he will dwell with them, and they shall be his people, and God himself shall be with them, and be their God. (4) And God shall wipe away all tears from their eyes; and there shall be no more death, neither sorrow, nor crying, neither shall there be any more pain: for the former things are passed away.*

"*And I heard a great voice out of Heaven saying, Behold, the tabernacle of God is with men.*" I'm not going to proclaim to be any great theologian in these matters but if a voice out of Heaven says something, this means to me that I must be standing below it. And the only thing below the heavens is the Earth. And when a city comes down out of Heaven, it has to land somewhere! And if God is with men, would it not seem reasonable to assume that He is with men where they reside, as on Earth? Listen, if your species name was "Angel" you would live in Heaven, but it's "Human" and like it or not, humans live on Earth and always will according to God. I understand the desire to get away from the awfulness, but God is going to put you right back here again. So eat your peas, whether you like them or not – they're good for you!

Two sides of the same coin

"I don't want to," and, "I don't have a choice," are the inscriptions found on each side of the coin of death. As long as you keep paying tribute to death, these sayings will keep ringing in your ears. What do I mean by tribute? Once again I call on Webster to define it as:

> **TRIB'UTE**, n. [L. tributum, from tribuo, to give, bestow or divide.]
>
> 1. An annual or stated sum of money or other valuable thing, paid by one prince or nation to another, either as an acknowledgment of submission, or as the price of peace and protection, or by virtue of some treaty. The Romans made all their conquered countries pay tribute, as do the Turks at this day; and in some countries the tribute is paid in children.
>
> 2. A personal contribution; as a tribute of respect.
>
> 3. Something given or contributed.

Tribute is paid to those who hold you in submission or bondage so they don't attack you. In modern day terms it's the same as protection money. It is based on the fear of what could happen to you if you didn't pay it. But let's look at what Jesus has done for us here also.

> Hebrews 2:14-16 Forasmuch then as the children are partakers of flesh and blood, he also himself likewise

*took part of the same; that through death he might destroy him that had the power of death, that is, the devil; (15) **And deliver them who through fear of death were all their lifetime subject to bondage. (16) For verily he took not on him the nature of angels; but he took on him the seed of Abraham.***

Whether you want to admit it or not you're a scare-dee cat. You're afraid of death. This tells me that you've never fully embraced the truth of God's Word on the matter. So you pay your tribute to the enemy with cloaked phrases and actions that display the fear which dwells within. You pay into life insurance policies, 401K and re-tirement accounts; attend health spas, beauty salons, and consult with plastic surgeons all in an attempt to hold back the ravages of a fear that you'll die. *"But I am getting old. I have downs where I used to have ups, flab where I used to have firm. I've got to provide for my family you know."*

I'm not going to tell you that you shouldn't do any of these things if this is what you believe. I'm merely pointing out that your intention reveals a fear of death. Let me ask you this: Would you ask God how old He is? Most answers to that question are "no" because we recognize that He is eternal. So as my daughter will often say, "What am I - chopped liver?" Are you made in His image and likeness or not?

Let me shift back to this generational mindset for a moment. How many of you have done some stunt which could have caused your death? There is presently a death-defying nature which permeates our youth simply because they are trying to push the limits of what they know about their world. Their intent is to challenge the common notion that things can't be done. These people live in a realm of their nature that is very close to the heart of God's Kingdom. When they have completed one of these stunts, they look into the eyes of a defeated foe and thumb their nose at him as a common salute to the demise of another mindset blasted out of their character.

Please don't, at this moment, allow that religious spirit to arise and make some comment like, "Well, what would you expect from someone who isn't saved?" I am talking about kids who are saved as well as those who aren't. They are closer to God's nature than you are right now. They at least believe in the impossible. Can you make this same claim, or have you been so beaten down by the products of your world colliding with the Kingdom of God that you've settled into a meager existence of just surviving. Could your life be a representation of the servant who buried the master's talent in the earth because you knew him to be hard task master?

Eternal Life.

Why a seed?

Have you ever noticed how much seeds are mentioned in the Bible? What's up with that? Everything is a seed it seems. Look at this as a reference. In my handy dandy Bible search program I can find 286 occurrences of the word seed or seeds. Now compare that with my name, Michael, which only occurs fifteen times! There are almost twenty times more references to this little device then there are to me. If this book is about me and my life, then how come there aren't more references to me in it? This is a point I've had to grapple with for some time now as you may have guessed, but I'm not going to go more into the subtle complexities of an over-worked imagination regarding this blatant disregard ... Excuse me.

What is a seed? Again using a ploy from Mrs. Thompson, a seed is:

> *1. The substance, animal or vegetable, which nature prepares for the reproduction and conservation of the species. The seeds of plants are a deciduous part, containing the rudiments of a new vegetable. In some cases, the seeds constitute the fruit or valuable part of plants, as in the case of*

*wheat and other esculent grain; sometimes the
seeds are enclosed in fruit, as in apples and melons.
When applied to animal matter, it has no plural.*

*2. That from which any thing springs; first principle;
original; as the seeds of virtue or vice.*

3. Principle of production.

*4. Progeny; offspring; children; descendants; as the
seed of Abraham; the seed of David. In this sense,
the word is applied to one person, or to any number
collectively, and admits of the plural form; but
rarely used in the plural.*

5. Race; generation; birth.

This is all very informative, but why a seed? Let's take a moment to look what Jesus has to say about this. (At this juncture many of you who have been trained up in the faith movement should already be zoning out because you know as a matter of indoctrination when ever the word "seed" is mentioned, you, out of reflex, turn to Mark 4. Well for your information the same passage is also in Matthew 13 and Luke 8.) Let's go to John 12.

> *John 12:24 Verily, verily, I say unto you, Except a corn of
> wheat fall into the ground and die, it abideth alone:
> but if it die, it bringeth forth much fruit.*

Why, you may ask, did I go there when every other instance of "seed thought" goes to the chapters I previously mentioned? We have to get away from the formulas of good "churchianity" and get back to the purposes of the Kingdom of God. Jesus

---

Eternal Life.

himself tried to put this across to those who He came in contact with. The basis of this passage comes at a monumental time in the ministry of the Man Jesus. Soon the culmination of His work would be complete, and the immediate result of that work would not be very appealing to the causal onlooker. The weight of this has begun to press down upon him and, just as every human does when faced with pressure, the heart speaks. What is so powerful here is the fullness of the Kingdom message is represented here from verses 23 to 34. So you don't think I'm making this stuff up, here is the entire passage:

> *John 12:23-34 And Jesus answered them, saying, The hour is come, that the Son of man should be glorified. (24) Verily, verily, I say unto you, Except a corn of wheat fall into the ground and die, it abideth alone: but if it die, it bringeth forth much fruit. (25) He that loveth his life shall lose it; and he that hateth his life in this world shall keep it unto life eternal. (26) If any man serve me, let him follow me; and where I am, there shall also my servant be: if any man serve me, him will my Father honor. (27) Now is my soul troubled; and what shall I say? Father, save me from this hour: but for this cause came I unto this hour. (28) Father, glorify thy name. Then came there a voice from heaven, saying, I have both glorified it, and will glorify it again. (29) The people therefore, that stood by, and heard it, said that it thundered: others said, An angel spake to him. (30) Jesus answered and said, This voice came not because of me, but for your sakes. (31) Now is the judgment of this world: now shall the prince of this world be cast out. (32) And I, if I be lifted up from the earth, will draw all men unto me. (33) This he said, signifying*

what death he should die. (34) The people answered
him, We have heard out of the law that Christ
abideth forever: and how sayest thou, The Son of man
must be lifted up? who is this Son of man?

In order to advance this seed discussion a bit further, I have
to put the beginning passage of seed criteria in here so that I can
reference it also.

Genesis 1:10-13 And God called the dry land Earth; and
the gathering together of the waters called he Seas:
and God saw that it was good. (11) And God said,
Let the earth bring forth grass, the herb yielding
seed, and the fruit tree yielding fruit after his kind,
whose seed is in itself, upon the earth: and it was so.
(12) And the earth brought forth grass, and herb
yielding seed after his kind, and the tree yielding
fruit, whose seed was in itself, after his kind: and God
saw that it was good. (13) And the evening and the
morning were the third day.

So, "Why a seed?" is the question we're looking at.
According to our definition, a seed deals with re-production, the
expansion of plant and animal life, the propagation of family
generations. When you talk about seeds this is what everyone
generally thinks about. Nothing wrong with this perspective, but
why is the Kingdom of God referenced so often around a seed if
God is eternal and life just comes from Him? This seems a little
redundant as a reminder. Let me postulate here that, according
to Jesus' own description in John, the real meaning of a seed is
not in the life it carries but in the death that it must subject itself

to in order to re-produce life. (Come on now, what is this book about?) Jesus even provides the instruction to obtain eternal life in this world, but I'm jumping ahead of myself.

We all know what a seed looks like. They come in a variety of sizes and shapes - just like people - and if you're like a child, you don't really know what it will produce until it is put in the ground, watered, and begins to sprout. What we neglect is that in the plant kingdom seeds appear only when death happens. In order for the seed to be complete, the parent plant which produced it must be dead. Take this back to the Genesis account and you'll see God is calling life back onto the earth which is void of any plant life. Notice how God declares in Genesis 1, verse 11 that the earth shall bring forth seed-producing plants, or another way of saying this is that the material of death shall birth life. Jesus confirms, according to John 12 in the 24th verse, this same principle, completing the cycle by stating that the corn has to fall to the ground and die.

Now seeds only do their best work when they are placed in the ground according to Jesus. This is pretty self-explanatory. You don't buy a packet of flower seeds and place the packet in a vase expecting it to suddenly produce blooms. God said, "No," to this type of thinking. Something has to be hidden from your sight and sensibility in order to produce the results He has intended. The seed has to be enveloped by the matter of death, placed under pressure and watered in order for the life written within it to spring forth.

Speaking of life, we must understand that every seed has written within it the code for it to do what needs to be done when the conditions are correct. It will sprout no matter what the conditions are which surround the seed to affect its fullest development. In Mark 4 (see, I had to go there sooner or later) Jesus describes the stony ground and the ground which chokes off the seed with thorns and thistles. The seed knows what to do; you can't tell it to stop doing its action once it hits the ground. But you can influence its result by the type of soil it is placed within. So let me take a brief excursion here as a way of illustrating my point. Go with me to another great seed scripture that most everyone has encountered,

> *Luke 17:5-6 And the apostles said unto the Lord, Increase our faith. (6) And the Lord said, If ye had faith as a grain of mustard seed, ye might say unto this sycamine tree, Be thou plucked up by the root, and be thou planted in the sea; and it should obey you.*

This same verse is in Matthew 17 and deals not with a tree but a mountain. What I like to think here is that this principle works on every type of condition: those which are temporal (the tree) and those that appear to have been around forever (the mountain). So let's break this down into the components. There is first the issue of faith; then there is the seed; next speaking to an object; and then there is what you want to speak (recall what you just read in the previous chapter); and finally, the accomplishment of the end result. Pretty fundamental, so what's the big deal you're asking? You've heard this taught every which way and still nothing seems to validate your experiences in life. You've spoken to everything in your life you've wanted thrown into the sea and nothing has changed. Your "little" mustard seed faith can't even be measured it's now so small. (As a side note here, there is a plant called a dust orchid that has the world's smallest seed. It requires over a million of them just to measure one gram! How small is your faith now?)

Remember what launched me into this track – seed codes. Faith as a grain of mustard seed. There is an association here. Does a mustard seed have faith? *"That is illogical!"* you're probably saying. This is the Kingdom of God we're speaking about here where man's logic doesn't have supreme rule. So I'll ask again, does a mustard seed have faith? I simply don't know according to human terms, but let me pose this. According to Hebrews it is impossible to please God without faith. Further, we know in Genesis 1:12 every plant produced seed and God saw that it was good. I would say according to these verses, that yes, a mustard seed has faith. Now comes the kicker: whose faith does it have, its own or God's? I would have to say that every seed, mustard, orchid, avocado, turnip or whatever you select, has faith and that faith is God's faith. He designed it and wrote into it the code for it to produce after its kind. When you throw seed down on the ground you are activating God's faith, or instructions, that the seed will sprout. It's God's faith which is on the line here, not the seeds. The seed doesn't wonder if it will sprout or not, it doesn't harbor some thought like, "Well I don't know if it's my time or not", or "This isn't what I'm used to", or "What will the other seeds think?" Come on folks! Seeds don't think, so why do you?

So let me paraphrase Luke 17:5-6.

> *Luke 17:5-6   And the apostles said unto the Lord, Increase our faith. (6) And the Lord* thinking to himself said, "Boy if these guys knew what the Father and I placed within them, they wouldn't need to ask me to increase their faith. If they understood that we, the Father, Holy Spirit and myself, decided that, in order for humans to rule and reign on this earth, their authority, expressed in mere words, would accomplish any task they set their heart to simply because we have faith that they can do it. But now they've allowed the adversary to twist their thinking and it has screwed up the link between their words and the creative nature that reside within them. I've already told them that they have the faith of God, but you have to keep repeating yourself until they hear it for themselves. So I've got to be careful how I word this because this could be a loaded catapult in the hands of a child if I don't ease them back into their right nature. I don't want them trying to rain fire down from Heaven again. So let's keep it simple and with the least amount of collateral damage to this planet." *If ye had faith as a grain of mustard seed, ye might say unto this sycamine tree, Be thou plucked up by the root, and be thou planted in the sea; and it should obey you.*

The Godhead has faith in you. They trust you. They think the world of you. You're pretty darn special in Their eyes.

They've crafted something very special in you that only you were designed to accomplish, no one else, not even me. You, and you alone. They believe in your purpose so much that They have given you as long as you need to fulfill it, and if you want, They'll give you something else, too. The only thing stopping you from doing it are the thorns of life.

AAAIIIGH! Weeds!!

If you've done any kind of gardening at all, you know weeds - those pesky little plants which seem to come out of nowhere and won't leave no matter what you try to do. I've spent an entire weekend rototilling the ground, removing all the weeds that came up last year, dumped new, fresh topsoil, raked it all out nice and smooth ready to plant my grass. Come back the next day and there are weeds! What gives? You know the story right? Come on; let's go back to Genesis 3. God puts man in the garden of Eden to till it and guard it. Along comes the enemy (which is merely a re-hash of past writings, yada, yada, yada ...), God curses the enemy and the woman, and then comes to Adam, which is where I'm going to pick up at.

> *Genesis 3:17-19 And unto Adam he said, Because thou hast hearkened unto the voice of thy wife, and hast eaten of the tree, of which I commanded thee, saying, Thou shalt not eat of it: cursed is the ground for thy sake; in toil shalt thou eat of it all the days of thy life; (18) thorns also and thistles shall it bring forth to thee; and thou shalt eat the herb of the field; (19) in the sweat of thy face shalt thou eat bread, till thou*

return unto the ground; for out of it wast thou taken: for dust thou art, and unto dust shalt thou return.

Headlines read: Cursed Ground – Thorns and thistles have a field day!

You've got to ask yourself, *"Self, weren't there any thorns and thistles up until that moment?"* A good question. Let's have Jesus answer it for us. (Yes, I'm going back to Mark 4, kinda.)

> *Matthew 13:22   He also that received seed among the thorns is he that heareth the word; and the care of this world, and the deceitfulness of riches, choke the word, and he becometh unfruitful.*

According to Jesus, thorns (and I assume thistles since they have thorns, too) are cares of this world and the deceitfulness of riches, which choke and makes one unfruitful. I'll bet you that up until Adam received the revelation that there really was something to what God said not to do, he didn't have a care in this world. Life was GOOOD! Then suddenly, *"How are we going to make it? Where will we live? We can't stay with her folks. What will the neighbors think of us? What will we eat? Oh no! I don't even know if she knows how to cook. And me. What is an out-of-work gardener going to do to support the two of us? Maybe I should go to school and learn a trade, but which one and how will we pay for that? Maybe they have a dorm that will permit us to live together... "*

Cares bombard your mind, not only while you're awake but while you're sleeping. You're tormented by all these and so many more, and guess what it's doing to you? Making you snake food. You read that right: SNAKE FOOD! Those cares of the world and its riches will drive you right back into the dust of the earth which is exactly what God said was to be the food of the snake. SNAKE FOOD. SNAKE FOOD. SNAKE FOOD.

Where will we live? SNAKE FOOD. How am I going to pay for this? SNAKE FOOD. What will they think ... SNAKE FOOD. The bank called about what? SNAKE FOOD. That's pretty darn depressing. SNAKE FOOD. Sorry, got carried away there, but it does make a point. Our thoughts have got to go.

> *Romans 12:2 And be not conformed to this world: but be ye transformed by the renewing of your mind, that ye may prove what is that good, and acceptable, and perfect, will of God.*

Now with all this talk about the power of thorns infiltrating our lives and removing us from the will of the Father's plan, you'd have to think there would be some way of overcoming this. Don't you re-member what Jesus thought in the paraphrased versus of Luke 17 from above?

> *Luke 17:6 Paraphrase "... they've allowed the adversary to twist their thinking and it has screwed up the link between their words and the creative nature that reside within them. I've already told them that they have the faith of God, but you have to keep repeating yourself until they hear it for themselves..."*

But fortunately for us the Father made a way to re-deem even our thought life if we'll only access it. And it's just like Him to make a spectacle of it for the whole wide world to see.

> *John 19:2-5 And the soldiers plaited a **crown of thorns**, and put it on his head, and they put on him **a purple robe,** (3) And said, Hail, King of the Jews! and they smote him with their hands. (4) Pilate therefore went forth again, and saith unto them, Behold, I bring him forth to you, that ye may know that I find no fault in him. (5) Then came Jesus forth, **wearing the crown of thorns, and the purple robe**. And Pilate saith unto them, **Behold the man!***

Behold the man! Another exchange that re-turned your authority to you. Beaten and battered, according to Isaiah, beyond recognition, a King wearing a purple robe, its color signifying the color of thistles and, a twisted crown of thorns around His head. His head bled with the placement of that crown upon Him; bled so the thoughts of the cares of this world would not beat you down and pulverize you with such force that you would forget that you are a king on this planet. Heaven is not your destination. You reign in this world. And the world has decreed loudly: I find no fault in YOU!

> *1 Peter 1:18-23 MSG It cost God plenty to get you out of that dead-end, empty-headed life you grew up in. (19) He paid with Christ's sacred blood, you know. He died like an unblemished, sacrificial lamb. (20) And this was no afterthought. Even though it has only lately--at the end of the ages--become public knowledge, God always knew he was going to do this*

for you. (21) It's because of this sacrificed Messiah, whom God then raised from the dead and glorified, that you trust God, that you know you have a future in God. (22) Now that you've cleaned up your lives by following the truth, love one another as if your lives depended on it. (23) Your new life is not like your old life. Your old birth came from mortal sperm; your new birth comes from God's living Word. **Just think: a life conceived by God himself!**

Eternal Life.

The Promise

Here are your choices: a) you can be a mortal or, b) you can be eternal. Before you chose let me provide an accurate description as Mrs. Thompson would.

MOR'TAL, n. Man; a being subject to death; a human being.

ETER'NAL, n. An appellation of God.

"But wait," some of you may be saying, "What's an appellation?" I recognize that Mrs. Thompson often was confronted with this same issue, using a word (or several for that matter) which I didn't know either. Being the expert that she was, she handled it in such an astonishing manner as follows:

APPELLA'TION, n. Name; the word by which a thing is called and known.

ETER'NAL, n. An appellation (name; the word by which a thing is called and known) of God.

"*But wait,*" some of you may now be saying, "*I am a human being. How can I be eternal and a human at the same time?*" Logic is not very becoming to you in the Kingdom of God. This is a realm where the impossibilities of man are possible. That is why we have a promise which cannot be broken.

Romans 4:13-22 For the promise, that he should be the heir of the world, was not to Abraham, or to his seed, through the law, but through the righteousness of faith. (14) For if they which are of the law be heirs, faith is made void, and the promise made of none effect: (15) Because the law worketh wrath: for where no law is, there is no transgression. (16) **Therefore it is of faith, that it might be by grace; to the end the promise might be sure to all the seed***; not to that only which is of the law, but to that also which is of the faith of Abraham; who is the father of us all, (17) (As it is written, I have made thee a father of many nations,) before him whom he believed, even God, who quickeneth the dead, and calleth those things which be not as though they were. (18) Who against hope believed in hope, that he might become the father of many nations, according to that which was spoken, So shall thy seed be. (19) And being not weak in faith, he considered not his own body now dead, when he was about an hundred years old, neither yet the deadness of Sara's womb: (20)* **He staggered not at the promise of God through unbelief; but was strong in faith, giving glory to God***; (21) And being fully persuaded that, what he had promised, he was able also to perform. (22) And therefore it was imputed to him for righteousness.*

Abraham was given a promise by God long before Moses came on the scene. That promise of being the heir of the world is still being fulfilled to this very day. Think about that for a moment. Despite what has gone on - and is presently going on - with the children of Abraham over all the millenniums, this promise from God is still in operation. No, it didn't stop with

Jesus either. You and I, our children, and their children are recipients of this same promise if you are in Christ. Let's take a look at Peter's take on this promise.

> *2 Peter 3:1-14 This second epistle, beloved, I now write unto you; in both which **I stir up your pure minds by way of remembrance:** (2) That ye may be mindful of the words which were spoken before by the holy prophets, and of the commandment of us the apostles of the Lord and Savior: (3) Knowing this first, that there shall come in the last days scoffers, walking after their own lusts, (4) And saying, Where is the promise of his coming? for since the fathers fell asleep, **all things continue as they were from the beginning of the creation.** (5) For this they willingly are ignorant of, that by the word of God the heavens were of old, and the earth standing out of the water and in the water: (6) Whereby the world that then was, being overflowed with water, perished. (7) But the heavens and the earth, which are now, by the same word are kept in store, reserved unto fire against the day of judgment and perdition of ungodly men. (8) **But, beloved, be not ignorant of this one thing, that one day is with the Lord as a thousand years, and a thousand years as one day. (9) The Lord is not slack concerning his promise, as some men count slackness; but is longsuffering to us-ward, not willing that any should perish, but that all should come to repentance.** (10) But the day of the Lord will come as a thief in the night; in the which the heavens shall pass away with a great noise, and the elements shall melt with fervent heat, the earth also and the works that are therein shall be burned up. (11) Seeing then that all these things shall be dissolved, what manner of persons ought ye to be in all holy conversation and godliness, (12)*

Looking for and hasting unto the coming of the day of God, wherein the heavens being on fire shall be dissolved, and the elements shall melt with fervent heat? (13) Nevertheless we, according to his promise, look for new heavens and a new earth, wherein dwelleth righteousness. (14) Wherefore, beloved, seeing that ye look for such things, be diligent that ye may be found of him in peace, without spot, and blameless.

I've just got to take this little detour. Look at verse 8 again, "Don't be ignorant." God does not measure time like we've been schooled. A twenty-four hour day for God equals 1000 of our earth years. So let me ask you a question: How old are you? Do you realize that if you are forty-two years old you have only been a lunch break for God? That's right, while you've been busy doing all this "growing up" stuff which has made you so all-fired important, God was kicking back having a sandwich and drinking a cool one. So why do you want to be mortal if your whole day in the eyes of God hasn't even happened yet? (You know this might fit the explanation of most people who say that they never have heard from God all their life: He's been out to lunch! I'm joking. You're so serious.)

I have heard from some zealous newbies rejoicing upon the anniversary of their salvation that they were "one year in the Lord." Do you realize to be that old, according to this verse we're talking about, you would actually be establishing yourself to be at least 365,000 years old! That is why, in verse 9, Peter wisely says the Lord is not slack as some might think. With a span of time amounting to a year in the eternal realm equal to 365,000 years in the earthly realm, you surely don't want to get you're human hopes up when God says, "I'll get back to you on that next week."

While I've got you thinking about durations of time here, let me talk about my least favorite subject: Time Management. I've spent a lot of energy here trying to get you to start thinking like God thinks and all of it can be wasted the minute you look at your day-planner. Let me get right to the heat of the matter: Time management principles deal from the perspective that time is scarce and you have to manage it effectively in order to accomplish all your goals to call yourself successful - or you die, which ever comes first. Do you see anything that even closely resembles Kingdom thinking here?

First, where do you come off thinking time will run out? You are eternal, right? Jesus said He came that you might have life and life more abundantly. Explain to me where there is scarcity in the word "abundantly." Next, show me how you manage time. To manage something means to control, manipulate, to direct. Do you really have that kind of ability? If you did, wouldn't it be easier to slow down time or even turn back time so you could achieve what you want. But the clock keeps moving forward at the same rate every day, and you can do nothing about it. Oh sure, Joshua was able to stop the movement of the sun in order to complete his battle with the enemy, but that required God's intervention to affect a cosmic law which He established. Joshua had to go into the eternal realm to do it, and I'll bet that he didn't have it written into his day planner:

3:30pm stop time to finish conflict

Lastly, your success is not, I repeat, is not determined by your self-determined goals. God said in Jeremiah that He knows the thoughts and plans He has for you, for a hope and a future. Your success is the completion of His thoughts and plan about you, not the other way around. That doesn't mean you don't have a part in it, you most assuredly do, but you measure what you do by His yardstick, not yours.

I bring this matter to your attention, not because I have an aversion to planning, but because it has become a twentieth-century tradition of man which makes God's Word have no effect in your daily lives. We're dealing with promises here, and God has given many of them to you concerning the very things you use your day planner to accomplish. Here is but one promise that cuts right to the heart of the matter.

> *Matthew 6:25-34 Therefore I say unto you, Take no thought for your life, what ye shall eat, or what ye shall drink; nor yet for your body, what ye shall put on. Is not the life more than meat, and the body than raiment? (26) Behold the fowls of the air: for they sow not, neither do they reap, nor gather into barns; yet your heavenly Father feedeth them. Are ye not much better than they? (27) Which of you by taking thought can add one cubit unto his stature? (28)*

And why take ye thought for raiment? Consider the lilies of the field, how they grow; they toil not, neither do they spin: (29) And yet I say unto you, That even Solomon in all his glory was not arrayed like one of these. (30) Wherefore, if God so clothe the grass of the field, which today is, and tomorrow is cast into the oven, shall he not much more clothe you, O ye of little faith? (31) Therefore take no thought, saying, What shall we eat? or, What shall we drink? or, Wherewithal shall we be clothed? (32) (For after all these things do the Gentiles seek:) for your heavenly Father knoweth that ye have need of all these things. (33) **But seek ye first the Kingdom of God, and his righteousness; and all these things shall be added unto you.** *(34) Take therefore no thought for the morrow: for the morrow shall take thought for the things of itself. Sufficient unto the day is the evil thereof.*

How many times has this passage been jammed down your throat in the prosperity message? And how many times have you said to yourself in disgust, *"Look preacher, that may be all well and good for you, but I have kids to feed and clothe, a wife who likes to have a roof over her head, and the only thing that I can do right now is go to my job and keep working to receive my paycheck to pay for these things."* This passage does not deny that you have these needs; it even admits they are relevant and God knows you have them, along with everybody else in the world. But this promise for God to give them to you (yes, He will give them to you) only occurs when you put in your day planner one priority and make it the top one and don't proceed to anything else until you've reached it. Seek first the Kingdom of

God and His righteousness. That is all you have to do. Simple, isn't it?

The dilemma is that there isn't a manual written for the Kingdom; which is why you have to seek for it. Additionally, since you probably need to be fed and clothed daily, you're going to have to seek for it daily, too.

Proverbs 25:2 It is the glory of God to conceal a thing: but the honor of kings is to search out a matter.

Before you go and get all religiously humble about how you're not a king, please realize, once again, it's not about you and your thoughts; it's about the thoughts and plans that God has for you. This is how He sees you, so start acting like it.

So let's get back to the promise. Peter talks about two promises in this passage which began my tirade: first, the promise of the coming of the Messiah; and second, the promise of the coming day of the Lord. While the main person in both of these promises is the same person, the conditions which Peter is referencing here are for two separate but identical occurrences. Verse 4 is Peter's recollection of the historical record the Jews had often expressed that the Messiah, or "Christ" in Greek, would one day come and deliver and relieve the entire state of Israel. This promise in one aspect has already occurred with Jesus, but Israel rejected the manner in which He came, so Israel still holds onto the thought that the Messiah is about to come for the first time. Hey! Peter knew better; he had been right there with Jesus and had witnessed all that God had done with and through Him. But the traditions of man still have to be overcome, and many of those traditions are made up by men who don't want to lose their influence over people, or as Peter says, "...walking in their own lusts." (What I find interesting here is that while talking about these two promises, there is a third implied promise that these types of people will get what's coming to them in the end!)

The second promise listed here by Peter is the results that occur when the end comes. Notice in verse 13 there is the promise listed of a "new Heaven and new Earth." I've been down this road already to some degree but I want to again get you off of this daydream you'll live in Heaven forever and ever. If that were to be the case then why does God need to create a new Earth again? He simply does it because, like it or not, He doesn't want you in Heaven with Him. Look at what it says in Revelation:

Revelation 21:3 And I heard a great voice out of Heaven saying, Behold, the tabernacle of God is with men, and he will dwell with them, and they shall be his people, and God himself shall be with them, and be their God.

"God is with men." Not the other way around folks. So let's get over it, okay?

So let's look at this promise which is the over-riding message of this book. I've mentioned it before, found in John 10.

John 10:10 The thief cometh not, but for to steal, and to kill, and to destroy: I am come that they might have life, and that they might have it more abundantly.

I don't think Jesus would have given this to us if He was not intent upon seeing it was carried out, do you? What I find intriguing is that He has associated abundant life with the works the enemy conducts against us in order to keep that life from us. Many will agree the enemy does all the things listed, but they won't accept that Jesus has given them something which counteracts the enemy's very nature right now, not some time in the future. What good is abundant life when you've allowed the enemy to kill you? But even this promise is reinforced by a passage in 1 John.

*1 John 2:21-25 I have not written unto you because ye know not the truth, but because ye know it, and that no lie is of the truth. (22) Who is a liar but he that denieth that Jesus is the Christ? He is antichrist, that denieth the Father and the Son. (23) Whosoever denieth the Son, the same hath not the Father: but he that acknowledgeth the Son hath the Father also. (24) Let that therefore abide in you, which ye have heard from the beginning. If that which ye have heard from the beginning shall remain in you, ye also shall continue in the Son, and in the Father. (25) **And this is the promise that he hath promised us, even eternal life,***

See eternal life is the promise. Yes, as the title of the book states, that means forever. God is not pleased when you die. He'll welcome you to Heaven but it's not going to be a long stay.

If you die (not when), you've allowed the enemy to declare that you're unable to please God according to His Word. Is that a harsh statement? Look at this passage:

Hebrews 11:1-6 Now faith is the substance of things hoped for, the evidence of things not seen. (2) For by it the elders obtained a good report. (3) Through faith we understand that the worlds were framed by the word of God, so that things which are seen were not made of things which do appear. (4) By faith Abel offered unto God a more excellent sacrifice than Cain, by which he obtained witness that he was righteous, God testifying of his gifts: and by it he being dead yet speaketh. (5) By faith Enoch was translated that he should not see death; and was not found, because God had translated him: for before his translation he had this testimony, that he pleased God. (6) But without faith it is impossible to please him: for he that cometh to God must believe that he is, and that he is a rewarder of them that diligently seek him.

The eyes of church people seem to glaze over whenever you open the "faith chapter" in a teaching because they've heard it used so much, for almost everything, that requires you to believe. This isn't a faith message; this is about eternal life and right at the middle of this passage, we are confronted with the all-time culprit of eternal life, Enoch. Theologians wish this guy would have died because he makes their lives so hard when they have to explain what happened to him. Well, it's simple; just read the text. He pleased God and God took him. This passage throws a whole mess of things into the air when those who don't believe in eternal life say that every man is appointed once to die and you say, "What about Enoch?" or better yet, "What about Elijah?" and if you really want to fry their circuits, "What about Lazarus?" Look, God was pleased with Enoch, plan and simple. There wasn't some law he fell under that he had to meet; there wasn't some offering he had to give; there wasn't some form of penitence which had to be exacted from him. Enoch found that if you search for God, it will please Him. If you search long enough and hard enough, God says, "Hey this guy won't leave me alone. Why not show him around the old Kingdom." POOF! Eternal life.

What will be your reward for diligently seeking God? A new house or car? Will your barns and vats overflow with abundance? How about fallen family members coming to the Lord? Will your body be healed of those debilitating diseases? All that is possible if this is what you're seeking Him for. But why don't you place your focus on the one lasting result which will put all of those things into a proper perspective. Eternal life – the process of living in the presence of God as He originally intended for you to live. That is your true destiny, so why not fulfill it now?

Finally; an eternal oxymoron

I have spent a lot of effort to try to get you to think differently about life. The hardest thing to do is to break away from the traditions we have set up. I honestly do not know how to get you to believe this Kingdom concept of eternal life simply because you have to experience the opposite of it in order to desire the bounty of an everlasting life.

I can't think of one person in this day and age who hasn't experienced the death cycle in one way or another. We all have had to deal with the loss of a loved one (even a hated one), but the death cycle is so much more than that. Consider the loss of hair or teeth, the loss of hearing or mobility. What about anything which is advertised on television that they claim you need to correct your present condition? This is the marketing of death to the masses at its worst.

Consider the demographical issues this planet currently faces. Experts say that Russia is in the midst of a population crisis. They are not replacing their population base with ne births. Their elderly are dying faster than children can be created. The people in power are trying to give incentives for young people to have children while they count down to the day of their own demise. They are concerned that in the next twenty years they could see a thirty-five percent reduction in their population.

This condition is also occurring all across Europe. Many of these countries are openly welcoming foreign nationals into their countries merely due to the foreigners propensity to have large family units that bolster the population base. But this has also come at a cost to national identity since many of this new population doesn't see or identify themselves as being from their new place of residence.

Conversely, in Japan, the opposite is happening. The social structure of the people in this island nation is very closely knit, and, subsequently, they don't willingly allow foreign nationals to live in their country. This unwritten policy has resulted in one of the oldest population bases in the world. Experts predict that in as little as twenty years Japan could lose as much as fifteen percent of its present population and even greater numbers after that. This doesn't even account for losses from natural disasters which this nation is susceptible to.

In the United States we face the largest transfer of wealth a nation has ever seen. This is the message the prosperity people have been expecting, but it's not what they thought. Presently, the baby-boomer generation is sitting on the largest asset base in this country. But this group of more than 76 million people, born from 1946 to 1964 representing almost one quarter of the

U.S. population, is also succumbing to the ravages of the death cycle. Consider that the growth industries in the next decade will be health care, pharmaceuticals, and yes, mortuaries as this body of people try to retain their bodies.

These are the natural realities of the death cycle that face each and every person on this planet. True, there are those individuals who believe this reduction in population is a good thing. But consider where in hell that thought even comes from. Death is not our original, God-given mandate.

These people will counter that the planet is running out of space for all the people and it cannot sustain it. Some "expert" has calculated that if every single person on this planet was to live in a house on a five thousand square foot lot, this singular community would be comparable in size to the state of Texas. Even if you were to take all of the world population and had them stand shoulder to shoulder, front to back, they would only cover and area the size of the city of Los Angeles. So even those that consider the reduction in world population as an acceptable solution live from the tree of the knowledge of good and evil.

Try to wrap your head around this thought. Many people fight for the right to die. Why not fight for the right to live as God intended us to live? Why after all did you commit your life to Jesus? So you could do a few good works and then let the enemy slap you in the face saying, "Wake up, fool. I'm still holding your passport to this planet and it's hereby been revoked!"?

*Romans 8:11 But if the Spirit of him that raised up Jesus from the dead dwell in you, he that raised up Christ from the dead shall also **quicken your mortal bodies** by his Spirit that dwelleth in you.*

Park your thoughts on this one verse and realize if you meet the one qualification that it lists, namely being filled with the Spirit, then your body will be made alive. This action is not a one-time deal – it is ongoing. This is the generator to your eternal life. Do you believe this? I'm serious; do you believe this one promise from God?

This is the greatest truth that God has ever tried to get across to us. Jesus said it is the truth that you know that will set you free. You must know this truth. You must become intimate with it, embrace it like a lover and hold onto it for, yes, dear life. We must never give in to the lie the enemy has placed before us which says your life is only to be a set number of years. Yes, I know others haven't been able to overcome this, but why does what they failed at affect you?

Look at the hall of faith in the eleventh chapter of the book of Hebrews again. There are only a few people listed there who "made" it. However, it clearly states that there is a whole other group of people who, while they didn't, receive the promise, are waiting for us to inherit it. So come on gang, we can't let them down, can we? Let's do this one for the Gipper! (I kinda got caught up in the moment there.)

Imagine what the worlds would be like if, as the Bible declares, there was a generation who lives and doesn't die. Consider all that could be accomplished if you didn't have to worry about running out of time. Or imagine how much attention you could give to a project knowing tomorrow will always be there.

Think about all the things you've put off simply because "you're too old." Imagine how much more enjoyable people would be without having to confront a "mid-life crisis." Picture what it would be like to have to rent a football stadium just to house your family reunion for just one side of your family!

I've reached the end of my campaign to get you to think differently. I honestly know that many of you will throw this down and go on with a life that is simply below what God has intended for you primarily because you don't want to take the effort to really change. If you're okay with that, then enjoy. It's neither right nor wrong; it is merely what it is to you.

I trust that some of the rest of you will have had the cobwebs of religion shaken out of your mind. Now you'll get the opportunity to examine the diet of death which had been, and is still being placed before you. Knowing the truth of a matter has a way of changing what you'll permit back into your life which had been "normal" before.

Lastly, to the remnant, those few hearty souls who are committed to the banner of eternal, everlasting life for God: Bravo! You are an inspiration to all who call on the name of Jesus. I hope to see you in a couple hundred years more vibrant and energized for the cause than you are today.

If any of you still think that there is a dignity in dying, then I would like you to define "dignity" in relation to a King who gave His life for you so that you could live forever. What dignity is there in not accepting His gift to you?

I close with the words of that great hero Buzz Lightyear, "To infinity, and beyond!"

Charis, chesed, and shalom to you.

Mike

About the Author

Mike and his family live in Portland, Oregon, where he is one of the teachers of the Word of God at a local fellowship in Clackamas, Oregon. As a graduate of the Latin University of Theology, Mike is passionate about people understanding what the Kingdom of God is, its impact in their lives and how it changes communities who are determined to operate from its authority.

Mike is the author of *Grace for Shame, Chesed: Beyond the Veil of Mercy, Your Life is a Freaking Mess and You Want Answers,* and *A Kingdom Primer.*   Mike also contributes his insights about the kingdom of grace at www.graceforshame.com and www.mygrace2u.com.

Mike can be contacted at mike@mikehillebrecht.com

Chesed
Beyond the Veil of Mercy

mike hillebrecht

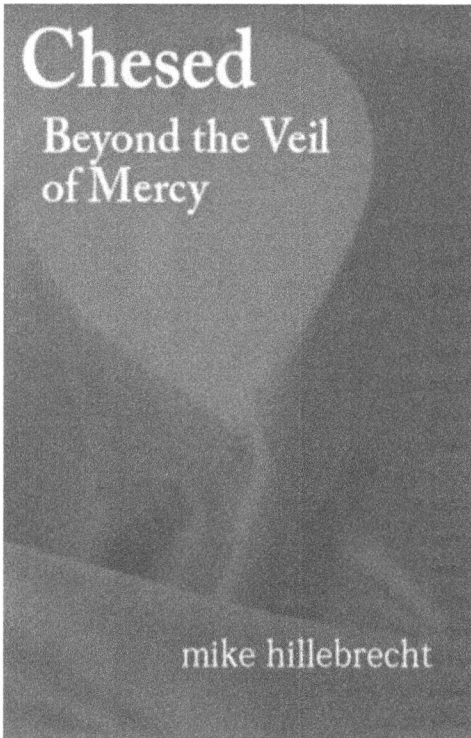

Additional titles by mike hillebrecht

What if what you knew from scriptures about mercy wasn't quite accurate? What if the blessings that we've been searching for have been locked away all this time in a simple Hebrew word that scholars agree has no English translation?

In this brief expose, teacher and author Mike Hillebrecht (Grace for Shame) explores the meaning of a Hebrew term that the original bible scholars may have interpreted inaccurately into the Greek word we know as "mercy." You will begin to see how many of the Old and New Testament passages take on an entirely different meaning by understanding this key Hebrew word in its proper context.

Mike will take you through a practical explanation of the full meaning of coming to the throne of grace in God's Kingdom not with the expectation of judgment but with the fullest measure of equality. This is an eye-opening study that will impact your walk with the Lord and those that are around you.

ISBN/EAN13: 0615617352 / 9780615617350

Page Count: 70

Trim Size: 6" x 9"

Language: English

Color: Black and White

Related Categories: Religion / Biblical Studies / General

www.beyondthemercyveil.com

Shame. Embarrassment. Humiliation. The ugly trio. Their distinct occupation is to keep you seeing yourself as a sinner saved by grace rather than as a son seated next to the throne of grace. The distinction is about whether you are being reigned over or whether you're reigning. It's a battle for your predestined role in the Kingdom of God.

Inside *Grace for Shame* you will discover a fresh look at what grace truly looks like and how God designed it to operate in your life. This ain't your papa or mama's grace - this is grace straight from the Kingdom of God as it has been operating throughout all of eternity. You will find the grace that is intended to break off the shackles that the ugly trio has bound you with, imprisoning you from your destiny.

Expect to finally identify with the true kingdom meaning of the cross - not the sanitized message that religion has produced. Are you considered a prodigal son, or know someone who is? *Grace for Shame* gives a perspective from the Kingdom of God that it's not about your past but about how truly great you are right now in the eyes of the Father.

ISBN/EAN13: 0615605508 / 9780615605500

Page Count: 220

Trim Size: 6" x 9"

Language: English

Color: Black and White

Related Categories: Religion / Christian Life / Personal Growth

www.graceforshame.com

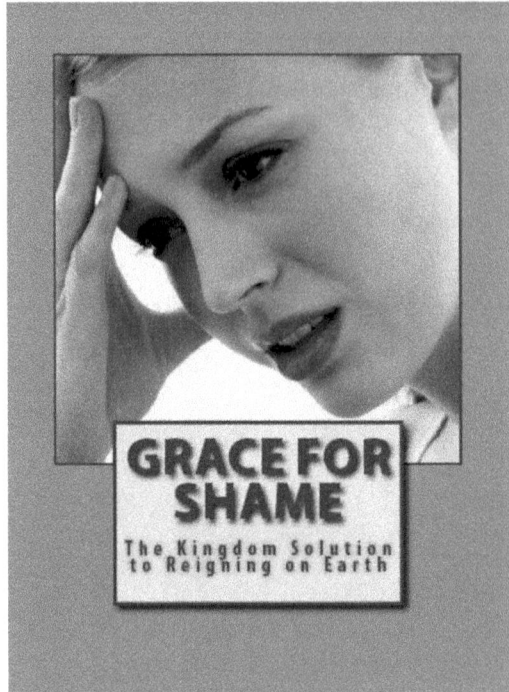

If you desire to be known as a Son of God according to Romans 8, you had better know the 3-R's of the Kingdom. They are the foundational tenets of the kingdom's interaction with you as a son. The Holy Spirit will not advance you to the head of the class if you miss any one of the important lessons these have to demonstrate. Within this booklet you will find covered the following items:

A KINGDOM PRIMER

THE BASICS OF THE KINGDOM OF GOD

MIKE HILLEBRECHT

The Father's intent – What was the original intent of God and how it changed.
Reconciliation – The Father's plan.
Redemption – The purpose of Jesus
Righteousness – The effect of reconciliation and redemption.
Right of Law – Where you are in God's time-line.
Royal Law – This is the one law given by the King.
Perfect Law – This is what we're striving to adhere too.
Peace – It may not be what you think.

As with the purpose of any primer, the entire spectrum of the topics offered cannot be presented to their fullest measure. This book is designed simply to be a building block which will provoke your thoughts about the matters at hand and spur you to search out further how they impact your walk with the Father.

Trim Size: 6" x 9"
Color: Black & White on White paper
Page Count: 126 pages

ISBN/EAN13: 061562099X / 978-0615620992
BISAC: Religion / Biblical Studies / General

www.kingdomprimer.com

Eternal Life.

www.ingramcontent.com/pod-product-compliance
Lightning Source LLC
Chambersburg PA
CBHW060303050426
42448CB00009B/1732